Faith Without Certainty

Faith Without Certainty

Liberal Theology in the 21st Century

Paul Rasor

SKINNER HOUSE BOOKS

BOSTON

Copyright © 2005 by Paul Rasor. All rights reserved. Published by Skinner House Books. Skinner House Books is an imprint of the Unitarian Universalist Association of Congregations, a liberal religious organization with more than 1,000 congregations in the U.S. and Canada. 25 Beacon St., Boston, MA 02108-2800.

Printed in the United States.

Cover design by Kathryn Sky-Peck
Text design by Sandra Rigney

ISBN 1-55896-484-3
978-1-55896-484-6

Library of Congress Cataloging-in-Publication Data

Rasor, Paul.
    Faith without certainty: liberal theology in the 21st century / Paul Rasor
       p. cm.
    Includes bibliographical references and index.
    ISBN 1-55896-484-3 (alk. paper)
    1. Liberalism (Religion)   I. Title.

BR1615.R39 2005
230'.046—dc22   2004028837

5 4 3 2
08 07 06

Contents

Introduction

LIBERAL THEOLOGY IS CHARACTERIZED by the belief that human religiousness should be understood from the perspective of modern knowledge and experience. It goes back just over two centuries. This is not very long in the Christian tradition and is but the blink of an eye in the larger context of human religiousness. Even in its short history, liberal theology, like other theologies, has suffered its ups and downs. A century ago, it was the dominant theological force in the West, and especially in North America. After a period of serious crisis, it has reemerged to again become a healthy current in the larger theological stream. It has not regained the prominence it once had and is not likely to do so in the future. Yet this is true of all other theological options as well, as theological pluralism has become the order of the day. But all in all, liberal theology is alive and well and remains one of several important theological options today.

At the same time, as we enter a new century, liberal theology must face several important issues. Many of these emerge out of the shifting historical circumstances that create the context for liberal theology's voices. Simply put, we live in a world today that is very different from that which witnessed the emergence of liberal theology two centuries ago. Several features of this new context, especially those gathered under the postmodern umbrella, have forced liberal theology to reexamine some of its deepest and most cherished beliefs.

Not all the challenges facing liberal theology today are from outside the tradition. Liberalism has generated several of its own crises over the years, and it continues to do so. Indeed, liberal theology has some critical tensions built into its very structure. These tensions cannot be resolved; they are simply inherent in the liberal religious worldview. Living with them is part of what it means to be a religious liberal. In different historical circumstances, these tensions express themselves in different ways. We will begin by describing some of the tensions and confusions among religious liberals today. These observations will form the points of departure for the analyses undertaken in this book.

For several years now, religious liberals have expressed a sense of unease in various ways. They are increasingly confronted with the tensions inherent in their chosen tradition, tensions that often are just below the surface. Sometimes these tensions emerge as people become aware of competing liberal values, which if not exactly contradictory, often pull us in more than one direction at once. A recurring example is the deep commitment to individual freedom, which can easily run up against a longing for a greater sense of community, perhaps even a desire for more guidance from or even accountability to a larger group.

Tensions often play out in the way religious liberals seek substantive truth. Liberals remain committed to such principles as free religious inquiry, autonomous judgment about truth claims, and openness to divergent views. At the same time, many also yearn for more shared content, for a common understanding about their faith that is more specific than what they have now. They don't want creeds. They remain committed to the principle of the individual search for truth and meaning, but they also want the search to lead somewhere.

This tension can especially affect newcomers. Many people come to liberal congregations to free themselves from what they often describe as the suffocating conformity of doctrine in other traditions. Yet once there, they sometimes find that the absence of a prescriptive belief system leaves them feeling adrift in the religious sea. Like others, they want to be able to respond with joy and conviction to the perennial question, "What do you liberals believe, anyway?" And they want to be able to do this without resorting to the tired liberal litany of things they *don't* believe.

Religious liberalism often involves a willingness to affirm faith without certainty. This is not the same thing as faith without conviction. It does mean that religious liberals tend to hold faith claims with a certain tentativeness. This is partly a result of a liberal mind-set that is always testing and second-guessing itself. It also reflects the liberal commitment to open-ended inquiry and the realization that truth is not given once for all time. This same tendency can produce personal belief systems or theologies articulated in generalized ideals, perhaps sincerely felt, but often without a deep grounding or much specific content.

Another tension can surface when religious liberals feel a need for more spiritual depth but find themselves reluctant to engage in the kinds of sustained spiritual practices that could provide it. Practices such as prayer and meditation on scripture may carry the negative weight of now-rejected childhood religious practices. Or they may be narrowly conceived in supernaturalistic terms or smack of pietistic and emotion-laden traditions that rational-minded liberals find uncomfortable. Of course spiritual depth may be found in many places, from nature to music to long-distance running, and many liberals (and others) find fulfillment along these spiritual paths. But if these practices are to become deep spiritual resources, they require discipline and regular practice. Liberals can fall too easily into the trap of thinking that the rational and the spiritual are opposing poles rather than mutually reinforcing parts of our human condition.

A similar ambivalence is sometimes present in our social justice work. Most religious liberals hold a vision of a more-just society and are committed to programs of social action that can help get us there. Yet they must also balance the demands of family, work, school, social life, and other commitments. Many are also sensitive to the privileges they may have—in education, wealth (or relative wealth), job security, health care—and don't want to give them up, even though they sense that a truly just society might demand some sacrifices. The result is often that our commitment to social justice, while deeply felt, can be hard to sustain.

This uneasiness among religious liberals reflects a set of tensions that lies at the heart of theological liberalism. We will explore these theological tensions with the assumption that they are not weaknesses. They are simply inherent in the liberal theology that undergirds our tradition. This book is in part an invitation to accept them and learn to live with them creatively. The deepest of these tensions relate primarily to issues around religious identity and to the liberal commitment to social justice. Both emerge out of the complex relationship liberal theology has always had to society and the larger culture. What follows is a framework for the discussion of these themes throughout the book.

At a basic level, the tension related to identity has to do with the difficulty of being able to say just who we are, religiously or theologically speaking. This tension is primarily a consequence of liberal theology's long practice of absorbing and adapting to the culture in which it is located. This mediating posture—turning to the natural sciences, social analysis, the arts, and other cultural sources—has enriched liberal theology in many ways, and liberals have long insisted that this is precisely what makes liberal theology credible and relevant. One of the by-products of this approach has been a tendency to blur the distinction between religion and culture. Critics of liberalism often charge that this stance amounts to an accommodation or even a capitulation of theology to culture. As a result liberals are in constant danger of losing their religious identity. Liberal religion then becomes indistinguishable from liberal politics or liberal social analysis, and spirituality tends to dissolve into pop psychology or New Age feel-good self-centeredness.

The traditional liberal emphasis on individual autonomy contributes not only to problems of individual identity, but also difficulties in sustaining group identity and denominational commitments. For example, liberals have often overlooked valuable resources from their own tradition ironically, however, their very insistence on individual autonomy is itself deeply rooted in tradition. When we insist too much on our own independence, it's easy to forget that we are still products of our cultures and that our worldviews come from somewhere.

Identity issues can also arise out of the liberal commitment to free and open inquiry and the liberal understanding that religious truths are not fixed. Liberals tend to hold religious ideas with a kind of open-endedness. They realize, for example, that experience can always be reinterpreted, that ideas and actions that seem good today may turn out to be misguided, and that particular religious doctrines are likely to change over time. One of the benefits of this stance has been to reduce the importance of doctrinal disputes among liberals. It can also make us reluctant to state with conviction who we are, which may be reflected in ambiguities around membership, among other things. Many liberal churches welcome long-term attenders as readily as official members, perhaps excluding them only from voting on by-law changes or the annual budget. This practice is not necessarily a weakness. Among other things, it reflects a deep commitment to inclusivity, also a mark of religious liberalism. Yet this open-mindedness can also make us reluctant to commit ourselves too deeply to anything, whether a belief or a plan of action, leading to a reluctance to commit to the liberal religious movement itself. Unfortunately, for many liberals depth is wrongly equated with narrowness. This brings to mind the warning offered by liberal theological ethicist James Luther Adams (1901-1994) many years ago that the liberal commitment to openness "can produce the mind that is simply open at both ends."

A different set of tensions emerges out of the liberal commitment to social justice. While liberal theology has always nurtured a deep involvement with contemporary culture, it has at the same time understood itself in prophetic terms as offering a critique of culture. Liberal theologians and religious leaders have been quick to call society to account in the face of injustice, to challenge the cultural status quo, and to work for reform. Adams called this the "progressive element" in religious liberalism.

Yet liberalism's connection with contemporary culture can also lead to soft or overly cautious religious stances, which can in turn blunt the edge of its social witness. Indeed, liberal theology's basic cultural orientation tends to produce a certain level of intellectual and social comfort. A related factor is the reality of social class. Religious liberals have tended to come from the educated classes of society and sometimes the ruling classes. In many ways they have often represented the very establishment they seek to critique. So while their theologies and religious principles often provide the justification for social reform, liberals have tended to avoid reform that is too radical. Put more starkly, liberals have historically resisted advocating any form of reform or justice that would require them to give up their own privilege. Critics of liberal theology, including many from within the tradition, often charge that these realities can easily make the liberal response to social justice issues inadequate or ineffective.

While this book is an exercise in liberal *theology*, it is also about liberal *religion*. These terms are not interchangeable, though they are obviously related, and they are notoriously difficult to define.

Fundamentally, religion has to do with the problem of finding meaning and orientation in life, one of the most basic human needs. While this need for meaning is present in each of us, it cannot be addressed exclusively—or even primarily—as an individual matter. Worldviews and other meaning-making frameworks are always given for us, in the first instance at least, by our cultures and our religious traditions. None of us ever starts from scratch.

Our religious traditions and practices help us orient ourselves in the world. They paint a large-scale picture of reality that attempts to explain the way things are and help us understand which things matter most in our lives and who we are in relation to the larger world. They help us to make sense of our lives in the grand context of the universe and the movement of history. They help give us meaning and purpose. They give us a place to stand.

Scholars in many different fields have long recognized a connection between religion and meaning. Psychologist James Fowler, for example, describes human beings as "creatures who cannot live without meaning" and deals at length with the development of religious faith as a response to this need. In anthropology, Clifford Geertz speaks of religion as providing "a framework of general ideas in terms of which a wide range of experience...can be given meaningful form." And theologians, of course, have long been concerned with this issue. Gordon Kaufman, for example, describes religion as "a sphere of culture within and through which humans [seek]...a sense of the meaning of human existence."

But what sort of meaning are we talking about here? What sorts of questions does religion address, and how are these questions (and their answers) different from the kinds of questions asked in other cultural spheres? We can begin by suggesting that religion is concerned with what we might call the Big Questions, questions about the meaning of life and death, how we understand our place in the cosmos, whether there is some ultimate reality to which we relate or belong, and so on. Different writers have articulated the framework for these questions in different ways. German-born theologian Paul Tillich (1886-1965), for example, speaks of "ultimate concern" or questions that address "the whole or human reality, the structure, the meaning, and the aim of existence." For American philosopher-psychologist William James (1842-1910), religious matters are those that have to do fundamentally with what he calls our "total reaction upon life" or our "attitude, whatever it may be, toward what [we feel] to be the primal truth." Similarly, American educator and philosopher Susanne Langer (1895-1985) speaks of religion as "a gradual envisagement of the essential pattern of human life." And theologian (and religious scholar) Richard R. Niebuhr has called religion "a kind of ligature by which we bind ourselves to divinity or that which bestows wholeness" and "by which we seek to bridge the distance that separates us from what is supreme in worth."

Religious ideas, symbols, and practices emerge as humans work out their cultural responses to these large concerns, and these provide meaning by producing pictures of the world and the human place within it. In other words, human life is, as Kaufman writes, "experienced as 'meaningful' when these conceptions and pictures are sufficiently convincing to provide a sense of purpose-fulness and value" in our lives.

Some examples may help. To begin, let's say that you believe the world was created by a loving God and that it has a purpose in God's plan. From this starting point, you might think of the world as moving in some general way toward a kind of ultimate re-demption, a place where God's perfect justice will eventually come to pass. In line with this, you might then think of human beings—including yourself—as created by God for the purpose of partici-pating in this larger plan. On a day-to-day level, you may struggle over how to make sense of realities such as natural disasters or child hunger in a world of plenty. Or you may struggle to under-stand tragic events in your own life, perhaps a crippling illness or the suicide of a friend. But your larger faith in God's plan gives you a context for these struggles. It gives you a way of looking at the world that has coherence and through which you can ulti-mately make sense of things.

Let's take a different example. You might think of the world or the universe as an evolving process that reflects ever-increasing complexity and interdependence. There may or may not be a grand purpose, but looking back you might discern some patterns and tendencies in this unfolding process. For example, the overall process might be one that favors life and the constant renewal of life. Or you might see history itself as one of these processes and think of history (especially human history) as moving toward some kind of goal or outcome, say a more just society or a certain harmony or stability. Within this worldview, you might see human beings as part of the unfolding process and therefore as moving within history to some sort of redemption or fulfillment. This too would give you a way of looking at the world that gives you meaning and purpose, although it might be a different sort of meaning than in the first example.

A third example: You might see this same evolutionary process as one that, instead of favoring life and renewal, favors or tends toward entropy and deterioration. In this context, you might see human history as moving toward chaos and dissonance, perhaps toward the kind of postapocalyptic society represented in movies such as *Blade Runner*. This worldview might lead to the belief that human beings tend toward evil or violence or destruction rather than toward good. You can see that if you held this basic worldview, your sense of life's meaning and your basic values and behaviors would be very different. But it would nevertheless give you a framework for meaning.

A final example: You might think of the universe as a random collection of matter and energy fields that have come together in various forms as a result of certain cosmic forces. From this starting point, you might think of life as a complete accident that has no particular meaning at all. The world has no larger purpose; it is evolving in the sense that these larger cosmic forces continue to operate, but it is not leading toward any particular outcome or fulfillment. Within this worldview, you might think of human beings as nothing more than one expression of these random processes with no intrinsic meaning of any kind. This would seem to make your own existence meaningless. But notice that this worldview also provides a way of orienting yourself in the world and offers a certain kind of meaning, a way of making sense of things.

The point is that we all live within these large worldviews. Indeed, these four perspectives can be found within the liberal theological tradition. We don't always think about them, make them explicit, or take the time to lift them to the surface and examine them—but they are there. We get them largely from our cultures and religious traditions, and more than one may be operating in our lives at the same time. Sometimes they are contradictory. Through this process, through the worldviews we are given and those we might create for ourselves, we develop a picture of the world and learn to know our place in it. We learn to trust the universe or to be suspicious, to think of it as basically good, or evil, or indifferent. We come to have ideas about what is really important and about what is of ultimate value. We come to have ideas about ourselves, not just each of us as individuals, but about human nature in general. Are human beings basically good and sometimes do bad things? Are they basically bad but sometimes do good things? Are human beings just biological organisms who seek only to satisfy their most earthly desires? Are they loving? Selfish? These are the kinds of questions religion and our religious traditions deal with.

Other dimensions of human culture may also provide a certain degree of orientation and meaning for life, and the different cultural spheres inevitably overlap. Politics and its symbols, for example, may provide a source of motivation and purpose, as may any number of activities concerned with working for greater social and environmental justice. Art and music may touch our deepest emotions and at the same time make us feel a part of something sublime, something larger than ourselves. Physics and astronomy often deal with large questions about the nature of the universe and the human place within it. In these and other ways, these pursuits reflect and respond to the human desire for meaning by providing what H. Richard Niebuhr called "centers of value."

In many ways, whether a particular activity or symbol is understood as religious is largely a matter of interpretation or circumstance. Our symbols are not inherently religious; objects and ideas become religious as religious meaning is assigned to them. Moreover, our contemporary world permits a wide range of interpretations. Some people look up and see the heavens where others see only astronomical objects (and some see both), and prophets as well as politicians speak of justice.

These different interpretive possibilities don't necessarily encompass the same level of meaning. As much as they may overlap, religion is concerned with particular kinds of questions about human life and death that other cultural spheres tend to ignore or take for granted. Further, all of these overlapping contexts within which we live, including religion, share the risk of producing self-serving or otherwise incomplete meanings. But the nonreligious spheres, precisely because their self-defined tasks involve a narrower compass, seem at greater risk. They can therefore fall short in their meaning-making activity, perhaps by suggesting a framework that is so human-centered that it fails to connect with something larger, or by painting such an impersonal picture of the cosmic order that it offers no real sustenance. A religious perspective pushes us toward deeper levels of meaning.

It is also important not to lose sight of the emotional dimension of our meaning-making activities. Our most important beliefs and values are always wrapped in emotions. We get upset or excited over things we care about, things that matter to us. If we are to find meaning in our religious ideas and symbols, it is essential that they not only make sense intellectually but also sit well emotionally. If they do, we can accept our worldviews with a degree of comfort and satisfaction. If our intellectual conceptions of reality don't feel right, whatever meaning they give us will be incomplete.

At the same time, while religious meaning is different from (although it overlaps with) the meaning offered by science and other cultural contexts, our religious understanding of the world and our place in it must also make sense in light of our contemporary scientific understanding of the universe. A long-standing principle of religious liberalism is that our religious meaning-making structures should not be isolated from the other cultural currents that flow alongside them. Only in this wider context can religion continue to speak to the real needs of people in their contemporary situation.

The term *theology* is often associated with arcane and academic or technical concepts that focus on abstract doctrines. But the purpose of theology is really quite simple. If *religion* is about the large-scale world pictures that orient us in the universe and help give our lives meaning and purpose, then *theology* is about examining these worldviews and the assumptions that go into them. It is about making our implicit patterns of orientation explicit, lifting them to the surface and examining them intentionally, honestly, and critically. It is about reflecting on these patterns, trying to make sense of them by questioning, clarifying, and rearticulating them. As Kaufman puts it, theology involves the "careful criticism and systematic reconstruction" of our worldviews, along with the symbols that support them.

Theology is not only about examining our ideas, but about examining our actions in the world and our justifications for them. That is, theology is (or should be) concerned as much with practice as with belief. This includes the internal practices of our congregations and faith communities, the daily habitual activities of our individual lives, and the larger social and institutional structures that make up our culture. All of these are grist for the theological mill; all are important subjects for critical reflection and analysis.

Theology is not done only by academics and religious professionals. This is work that all of us can do and that most of us in fact do, at least part of the time. Whenever we think about things that matter in our lives, whenever we struggle with tragedy in our families or express outrage at social injustice, we are doing theological reflection. Our struggle and our outrage are always grounded somewhere.

Liberal theologian Sallie McFague has made the following helpful observation about the role of theology:

> Thinking theologically is not an end in itself; it is for the purpose of right action, for discipleship.... Theology is therefore essential, even though it is not the central enterprise of the [religious] life. The goal of theology, as I see it, is to be *functional*, that is, to actually work in someone's life. It is meant to be an aid to right living, the supposition being that

examining one's beliefs (which may be only implicit, perhaps even chaotic or inconsistent) is necessary to acting thoughtfully and persuasively on the issues facing twenty-first-century Christians.

McFague's comments suggest that to be worth bothering about at all, theology has to satisfy two basic criteria: It has to make sense and it has to make a difference. That is, our worldviews—including our understandings of God, creation, human nature, evil, and so on—need first to be credible and coherent. They don't need to be systematic or especially sophisticated or even fully worked out. They do need to be something we can feel right about with a certain degree of intellectual integrity. And whatever the intellectual content of our theologies, they need to help us live properly in the world. They need to matter.

Finally, we need to remember that theology is never neutral and never universal. We always start from who and where we are, including our psychological makeup and our social location. This means that if we religious liberals are primarily a white middle-class group, our theologies need to acknowledge this and speak to our own condition. We will speak *from* our own condition whether we are aware of it or not. We certainly have to be aware of other perspectives, many of which are critical of liberalism. For example, at various points in this book, ideas from liberation theology are presented precisely because liberation theology speaks from the "underside" of history and offers perspectives on issues, such as poverty and oppression, that we might otherwise miss. This is especially important as we respond to social problems. To be in solidarity with those who are oppressed requires empathy and imagination. But no matter how much we identify with the poor, we can see the world only with our own eyes.

At the same time, theology always takes a stand, even when it seems to be operating in a purely descriptive mode. That stance may simply be one of reinforcing or reclaiming one's own tradition. It may implicitly support the status quo through its silence about it. Or it may draw on the resources of one's faith tradition to critically engage or critique important social issues. McFague reminds us that one of the theologian's most important roles is "to bring the perspective of the Christian faith to bear on the current and pressing issues of our day." This task is not just for professional theologians or indeed just for Christians. We all do this to some extent whenever we make moral judgments about issues such as poverty or education or war. As theologian Harvey Cox has said,

> Theology is unapologetically *pre*scriptive. It does not claim to be value-free or neutral. Theologians draw upon the beliefs of a particular tradition to suggest a course of action, an appropriate response, a way of life commensurate with what the faith teaches. Theology can be wrong; it cannot be noncommittal.

Theology is not something we do just with our heads. We must also use our hearts and guts, as well as our hands and feet. A more formal way of saying this is that theology involves the interplay of three dimensions: the rational/intellectual dimension, the emotional/spiritual dimension, and the practical/lived dimension. As McFague puts it, "thinking, doing, and praying belong together."

We might think of the intellectual dimension as the "naming" function of theology. As we struggle with theological ideas, we are likely to be involved in working out conceptual categories, coming to grips with the meanings of such key terms as *God* or *evil* or *salvation*, and perhaps trying to find a useful label we can use to name our own approach. And labels can be useful for lots of purposes. We are often subtly encouraged to reduce our theologies to a handy label by things like denominational surveys that ask us to describe ourselves by selecting one or more items on a list, such as humanist, theist, naturalist, pantheist, Christian, pagan, and so on.

These labels do tell us something. Even though our understanding of each of them may differ, they draw minimal descriptive lines within which we see ourselves and with which others in our tradition may partially identify. They also have their limitations. Naming your theology, identifying yourself within a particular theological orientation, involves more than labels. For example, saying that you are a theist doesn't really say much about the nature of the God you affirm. Is it a personal being? Does it have a gender? Is it an impersonal creative process? If so, what does it create? What powers or influences does it have? Is it purposeful? What is its relation to the world? To human beings? Similarly, saying that you are a Christian doesn't by itself explain how you think of Jesus or how much authority you give to biblical teachings. Even calling yourself a humanist or an atheist doesn't say much about you. To understand your theology, others need to know things like: What sort of God do you reject? Do you find any directionality or purpose in the universe or in evolution? What sorts of normative claims do you make about the way society should be structured, and where do they come from? Saying you affirm justice for all is nice, but what social arrangements count as just, and who gets to decide? These are important questions in any theology.

Another question is: How convinced are you? How deeply do you identify with the label you use? Doubt is always an inherent part of faith, and theology should never be free from doubt. Religious liberalism has always to some extent involved faith without certainty. German theologian Dorothee Sölle has pointed out that faith without doubt is not stronger, it is simply more ideological. The more important question is, How does your theology matter in your life? Is it something you affirm only in your head or also in your heart and in your guts? This leads to the second dimension of theology, the emotional/spiritual dimension. It is here that we begin to move from simply naming to truly owning our theologies.

At different times in our lives, we may sense a disconnection between our rational understanding and our emotional needs. This is worth paying attention to. What we long for is a theology that both makes sense and feels right. Until we find this, we haven't finished our naming process. And when we do finally get the intellectual and spiritual dimensions in sync, our theology becomes not just a label but a resource, a grounding for spiritual practice, for social critique, even for healing.

A complete theology involves not only thinking and feeling but acting. The way we live our lives names our theologies more effectively than any label we can give them. If we name a theology of love but treat people with disrespect, if we name a theology of interdependence but insist on our own independence, if we name a theology of inclusion but think we need to make all the important decisions, we are out of sync.

This works the other way around too. When we participate in an antiwar demonstration, when we write a letter protesting inadequate health care, when we go to work in a shelter or a youth program in the city, when we sit at the side of someone in pain, we are living and naming our theologies. The things we do, the things we go along with, the things we are silent about, these are all a part of the faith we name and practice.

But there is a danger here. How we live our lives may be the most telling form of naming our theologies, but stopping there leaves them incomplete as well. To say, "I live a good life, therefore I don't have to think about theology" leaves the process unfinished. It easily becomes an excuse to avoid articulating the basis for one's actions. From a theological perspective, it is important not only to live one's life doing justice and practicing kindness and love, but also to know why. Part of the task of theology is to articulate the religious underpinnings and moral principles that support our actions. It may be as simple as the biblical commandment to love God by loving our neighbors, or as complex as seeking to align ourselves with the creative force that draws the evolving universe toward greater interdependence, or as straightforward as trying to live out a particular vision of a just community or human fulfillment. Whatever it is, the task of theology is to help us name these principles and to say how our actions relate to them.

In the end, however we define it, it is important to recognize that theology involves many dimensions. It is a realm of feelings and actions as well as a realm of ideas. And this means that theology is hard work. It involves our whole selves—our heads, our hearts, our guts, our hands, our feet.

This book addresses several issues facing liberal theology today. It is both descriptive and critical. While some chapters emphasize one more than the other, these tasks are merged throughout. At the descriptive level, the book provides a basic introduction to liberal theology by describing its basic characteristics and locating it within its historical, intellectual, and social context.

At the critical level, the book continues an important feature of the liberal tradition by offering a constructive self-examination. At times it brings liberal theology into conversation with other theological approaches that are critical of liberalism. While liberal theology need not adjust to all its critics' complaints—it could not remain *liberal* if it did—there is much we can learn from them. In other cases, this book addresses a few of liberalism's home-grown weaknesses and contradictions, discusses why some of liberal theology's most deeply held ideas are problematic today, and offers constructive alternatives. It also addresses head-on the difficult issues of race and class that continue to confront liberal theology and sometimes cause us to stumble over our own best intentions. On the other hand, liberal theology has great strengths, such as its sincere open-mindedness, its emphasis on clear thinking, and its commitment to social justice. These are among the hallmarks of the liberal tradition (though it is worth remembering that liberals aren't the only ones who share them), and they are worth preserving.

The intended audience for this book includes clergy, theological students, and interested lay people who want to gain better insight into the liberal religious tradition. While it reflects my own Unitarian Universalist and Quaker experience, it addresses the broader liberal theological tradition. I believe the book will speak not only to Unitarian Universalists and liberal Quakers but to mainline Protestant Christians, modernist Roman Catholics, post-Christians and religious humanists, and others.

Organizationally, the book moves from the descriptive to the critical. The lines, however, are not sharp. The next two chapters discuss the basic characteristics of liberal theology and its philosophical roots. The following chapter starts from a different perspective. It asks, "If liberal theology is a child of modernity, what happens as we move from a modern to a postmodern cultural condition?"

The middle two chapters offer in-depth analyses of two critical issues in liberal theology today, its individualistic view of the self and its understanding of the relationship between language and religious experience, and suggest ways of understanding and constructively responding to these challenges.

The book finishes by dealing directly with liberalism's tensions around social justice, class, and race. One chapter takes up liberation theology's critique of liberalism; the other examines the continuing challenge of racism for liberal theology. In both chapters and throughout the book my goal is to better understand and respond to the dilemmas we face and to create new possibilities for strengthening the liberal prophetic witness in the world.

The Liberal Religious Mind-set

WHAT IS LIBERAL THEOLOGY, and where did it come from? What distinguishes it from the other types of theology being written and practiced today? These complex questions do have answers, and this chapter offers one approach to answering them. At the basic level, we can say that liberal theology is based on the premise that human religiousness should be understood and interpreted from the perspective of modern knowledge and modern life experience. It has been said that liberal theology tries to articulate a framework within which one can be deeply religious and fully modern at the same time. From this orientation, liberal theology is characterized by commitments to free and open intellectual inquiry, to the autonomous authority of individual experience and reason, to the ethical dimensions of religion, and to making religion intellectually credible and socially relevant.

Liberal Roman Catholic theologian David Tracy captures this perspective when he describes the liberal theologian as one who "accepts the distinctly modern commitment to the values of free and open inquiry, autonomous judgment, [and] critical investigation of all claims to scientific, historical, philosophical, and religious truth."

We need to be careful when making these general claims, however. For one thing, these commitments are expressed and

1

balanced in different ways by different theologians and in different historical periods. These are tendencies, not rigid criteria. Also, naming these as liberal commitments does not mean that liberals are the only religious people concerned with them. Many theologies that intentionally reject the label *liberal* engage in rigorous critical analysis and offer important social commentary. Nevertheless, liberal theology does reflect these central commitments.

These commitments are a part of what we might call the liberal religious mind-set. This is a helpful reference point because it describes the spirit with which liberal theologians approach their task. Seventy years ago, Rufus Jones (1863-1948), the great religious scholar and Quaker mystic, recognized this when he observed that "liberalism is first of all a spirit, an attitude, a state of mind." But what sort of spirit? We can begin with the word *liberal* itself. Derived from the Latin *liberalis*, its root is *liber*, or free.

The Oxford English Dictionary defines *liberal* as "free from bigotry or unreasonable prejudice in favour of traditional opinions or established institutions" and "open to the reception of new ideas or proposals of reform." Right away we see that the liberal spirit seeks to be not stuck in the past. Liberals tend to think of themselves as not bound by tradition but rather as forward-looking and reform-minded. Liberal theologian and social ethicist James Luther Adams put it this way: "Liberal religion by its very nature has aimed to live on the frontier and to break new paths." In this sense, the liberal attitude is a kind of mirror image of the conservative, which in its roots simply speaks of a tendency to preserve what is important from the past, to conserve.

In the religious context, the Oxford English Dictionary tells us that *liberal* is often applied "to those members of a church or religious sect who hold opinions 'broader' or more 'advanced' than those in accordance with its commonly accepted standards of orthodoxy." Presumably, we can read the term *advanced* here to mean "forward-looking" and not necessarily "superior." The distinction from *orthodoxy* also suggests this. Indeed, much of the history of liberal Christianity in the United States reflects a tendency to define itself in opposition to orthodoxies of every stripe, whether of doctrine, church organization, or social ethics.

Another aspect of the liberal religious spirit is a commitment to keeping an open mind, which includes a commitment to critical inquiry and intellectual freedom, qualities we see constantly in liberal theology. Liberals may hold strong opinions, but they rarely think they, or anyone else, have the whole or final truth.

Historical Sketch

A brief historical overview of liberal theology will provide some reference points for themes developed later in this chapter, as well as for the critical issues taken up in later chapters.

It is helpful to think of five basic "moments" in the history of liberal theology. These are not so much separate historical periods as nodal points, moments when we can see that something has shifted. These five moments are the precursors of liberal theology in the mid-eighteenth century; the true beginnings in the early nineteenth century; a period of prominence in the late nineteenth and early twentieth centuries; a crisis period, followed by a regrouping in the mid-twentieth century; and the emergence of new approaches in response to new challenges for liberal theology today.

PRECURSORS. Liberal theology is largely a product of the Enlightenment, which reached its peak in the eighteenth century and is commonly referred to as the Age of Reason. The element of reason is the dominant characteristic of the proto-liberal theology of the eighteenth century. This tendency was seen most prominently in the emergence of deism and other forms of so-called "natural religion." By stressing the role of human reason in the discernment of religious truth, the deists and their cohorts challenged the traditional emphasis on divine revelation.

The Enlightenment had an important effect on several New England ministers. The most important figures in this early liberal movement were Charles Chauncy (1705-1787), Jonathan Mayhew (1720-1766), and Ebenezer Gay (1696-1787), all of whom were pastors in Congregationalist churches in or near Boston. Reacting largely against the emotionalism of the mid-eighteenth-century revival movement known as the Great Awakening, these ministers preached a form of religion that stressed human moral capacities and the role of human reason and free will. They challenged the Calvinist doctrines of original sin and divine election, which they saw as denying the possibility and the motivation for living a moral life. In these and other ways, these eighteenth-century figures "laid the groundwork for a liberal alternative to orthodox Calvinism."

BEGINNINGS. It is commonly said that the great German theologian and philosopher Friedrich Schleiermacher (1768-1834) is the "father" of liberal theology and that liberal theology proper begins with the publication of his first book, *On Religion: Speeches to Its Cultured Despisers*, in 1799. Schleiermacher is one of the towering figures in the history of Christian theology. His work has had a lasting impact on liberal theology, particularly his conviction that theological claims must be consistent with other areas of human knowledge. As religious historian Claude Welch puts it,

> For Schleiermacher the only possible Christian theology was a 'public' theology, one whose warrants could be made clear and whose statements would be intelligible outside the bounds of the believing community. Those statements must also not be in conflict with other, nontheological claims to truth.

Following Schleiermacher, German theologians remained in the forefront of liberal theology throughout the nineteenth century. Many American theologians and religious leaders were influenced by them, especially in the late 1800s. Yet even in the early decades of that century, the liberal theological impulse was finding expression in the United States quite independent of German developments. Following the rationalist leanings of the eighteenth-century pastors, this new movement emerged primarily within the liberal wing of New England Congregationalism. Many within this movement accepted the label *Unitarian*, originally applied as an epithet by their opponents. As a result, the Unitarian movement became the primary "vehicle and testing-ground for liberal religious ideas" in the United States. During this formative period, the liberal movement's "unrivaled spiritual leader" was Unitarian minister William Ellery Channing (1780-1842). This early liberal theology understood itself primarily in contrast to the Calvinist orthodoxy of New England Puritanism. It blended a rationalist and an experiential approach to religion, and doctrinally it emphasized divine benevolence and human goodness.

In contrast to the situation in Germany, the key figures in the emerging American liberal theology were ministers rather than academics, and the pulpit was the primary locus of the new theological liberalism. Gary Dorrien, an Episcopal priest and historian of liberal theology, notes that while "American liberal theology was considerably less scholarly and systematic," it was also rhetorically a "more interesting, colorful, and spiritually moving tradition than its academic German counterpart." Theology did not become primarily an academic enterprise in America until the late nineteenth century.

RISE TO PROMINENCE. By the end of the nineteenth century, many liberal ideas that seemed novel or even radical two generations earlier had become widely accepted among American Protestant churches. The marginal had become mainstream, and liberals now dominated American theology. The many reasons for this shift included the impact of Darwinian evolution, widespread social unrest, an increasingly industrialized economic order, and the growing influence of biblical and historical criticism. The social gospel movement, which reinterpreted the gospel message in social terms, had become the hallmark of mainstream Protestantism and contributed to an emerging belief that American society was itself a vehicle of God's immanence. A sense of self-confident optimism and inevitable progress dominated the spirit of the times.

Two important shifts in the theological establishment are worth noting. First, liberal theology was no longer an exclusively Unitarian or liberal Congregational phenomenon. By the end of the nineteenth century, liberalism was truly ecumenical. All mainstream Protestant denominations participated in the social gospel movement, and the most influential American theologians and religious leaders now included Presbyterians, Episcopalians, Methodists, American Baptists, and Quakers, among others. The leading theologian of the movement was Walter Rauschenbusch (1861-1918), a Baptist. Ironically, perhaps, only one of the major social gospel theologians was Unitarian, Harvard's Francis Greenwood Peabody (1847-1936).

Second, while the liberal movement remained primarily a product of the churches during most of the nineteenth century, with prominent pastors its most important spokespersons, the main locus of liberal religious thought was shifting to the academy by the end of the century. Liberals were appointed to key posts at several leading seminaries, including Union Theological Seminary in New York City, the University of Chicago Divinity School, Boston University School of Theology, and Colgate Theological Seminary in Hamilton, New York. Harvard had been nominally Unitarian since 1804, although many observers have noted that during the early and middle decades of the nineteenth century, the most creative liberal theological thinking had come from the pastors it trained rather than its faculty. At the end of the century, Harvard Divinity School continued to be a liberal and largely Unitarian institution. But liberalism was spreading to other academic institutions. As a result, by the turn of the twentieth century, liberal theology had become the "new academic orthodoxy," as Dorrien puts it, "a field-dominating movement that redefined the religious teaching and social ambitions of mainstream American Protestantism." Religious historian Sidney Ahlstrom calls this the "golden age" of American liberal theology.

CRISIS PERIOD. The prominence liberal theology enjoyed at the beginning of the twentieth century was not to last. As Dorrien notes, the liberals' "sweeping optimism and success set them up for a hard fall." Theologically, of course, liberalism was never the only game in town, even when it was dominant. Conservatives of various stripes continued their critique, evangelism continued to flourish on American soil, and fundamentalism was beginning to emerge. More significantly, critiques of liberalism began to be heard within liberal environs. As the new century unfolded, however, the most serious challenge to the liberals' optimistic theological worldview was the rush of world events that clearly pointed in a different direction, events that could not be explained on the basis of liberal doctrines such as progress and divine immanence. This theological wake-up call began with World War I and the rise of fascism in Europe, followed by the Great Depression, World War II, and the horrors of the Holocaust.

The most important theological challenge came from a group of thinkers led by Karl Barth (1886-1968) in Europe and Reinhold Niebuhr (1892-1971) in the United States. The theological movement they spawned challenged the most cherished liberal tenets, and within a remarkably short period, it toppled liberal theology from its place of prominence. This movement is usually known by the term *neo-orthodoxy*, although several scholars have offered other terms, including *Christian realism*, *neo-Reformationism*, and even *neo-liberalism*. Its followers mounted attacks along several theological fronts, the most important of which were related to the liberal doctrine of divine immanence and liberalism's elevated view of human nature. From this perspective, the liberal understanding of sin and evil was completely inadequate, and the liberal tendency to locate God in human cultural movements was simply wrong. The neo-orthodox critics wanted to reestablish God's transcendent sovereignty and return human beings to their proper, fallen place.

Dorrien, among others, argues that this movement is best understood not as fundamentally different from liberalism, but as a much-needed corrective from within liberalism. However, many of the charges were overblown and unfair. Several liberal theologians did, for example, address questions of sin and evil, and not all liberals saw unlimited progress. Nevertheless, during the middle decades of the twentieth century, the neo-orthodox movement became the dominant theological force in America. Liberal theology did not disappear in the wake of the neo-orthodox challenge, though there were many who seemed ready to pronounce its demise. It did, however, find itself somewhat chastened, struggling to regroup and rethink its central theological claims.

TODAY. Beginning around 1970, a wide range of new types of theology emerged. With reference to liberalism, we can see two basic groups. To the left of liberal theology are liberation theologies of various types, including many feminist theologies. To the right are postliberal, communitarian, and other conservative theologies. There has also been a resurgence of liberal theologies, including process and relational theologies, political theologies, theologies focusing on the relationship between religion and science, ecological theologies, and more. As Dorrien puts it, "Today the liberal perspective in theology encompasses a wide spectrum of Christian and, arguably, post-Christian and interreligious perspectives."

Liberal theology today is healthy and robust. Dorrien's assessment notes,

> For all the critical pounding that it took in the twentieth century, often undeservedly, I believe that liberal theology has been and remains the most creative and influential tradition of theological reflection since the Reformation.

For all its strengths, liberal theology has not regained its position as the dominant American theology. Nor in today's postmodern cultural climate is it—or any other theological movement—likely to do so. The great variety of theological voices today means that liberalism must find its place alongside and in dialogue with many other approaches.

Different Strands

Liberal theology is most commonly associated with the rationalism that emerged out of the Enlightenment. But liberal theology has more than one source, and throughout its two-hundred-plus-year history, it has found more than one form of expression. In particular, the evangelical heritage of liberal theology is often overlooked. Dorrien expresses it well:

> Liberal theology is the child of two heritages. From its Enlightenment-modernist heritage it has upheld the authority of modern knowledge, emphasized the continuity between reason and revelation, championed the values of tolerance, humanistic individualism, and democracy, and, for the most part, distrusted metaphysical claims. From its evangelical heritage it has affirmed the authority of Christian experience, upheld the divinity and sovereignty of Christ, preached the need of personal salvation, and emphasized the importance of Christian missions.

The dividing line here has never been sharp. During liberal theology's formative years, these two strands were not separate at all. Key early American figures such as Channing and Congregational minister Horace Bushnell (1802-1876) drew on both their rationalist and evangelical roots, much as Schleiermacher had blended both the philosophical and pietistic elements of his German heritage.

By the early years of the twentieth century, however, the rational-modernist and the gospel-evangelical streams began to diverge as different thinkers emphasized one or the other approach. The leading figures of the social gospel movement, such as Walter Rauschenbusch, were clearly in the gospel-oriented evangelical camp. Meanwhile, a new form of modernist theology was establishing itself at the University of Chicago Divinity School, whose dean, Shailer Mathews (1863-1941), became the leading spokesman of the liberal movement. His book *The Faith of Modernism* (1924) was one of the most important liberal theological works of the period. Others within the modernist wing were venturing into distinctly post-Christian humanist territory. At the same time, a mystical form of theological liberalism, traceable to Ralph Waldo Emerson but finding new expression within liberal Quakerism and elsewhere, began to emerge. The leading figure in this strand of liberalism was Quaker mystic, scholar, and social activist Rufus Jones. Liberal theology no longer followed only one path.

Despite these new and seemingly divergent approaches, all forms of liberal theology continued to have much in common. They all retained the central commitments named earlier that allow us to define them as liberal. And while some scholars have drawn a sharp line between the modernist and evangelical groups, most recognize that nearly all liberal theologians have blended these heritages in some degree. The categories of "modernist" and "evangelical" are problematic for other reasons as well. It is worth remembering that whether they are rationalists, evangelicals, or mystics, all liberals are modernists. The commitment to linking religious life to the modern world is perhaps the central characteristic of liberal theology, whatever one's particular approach. Moreover, today the term *evangelical* has taken on a range of distinctly nonliberal connotations that probably render the term unsuitable, though it might be worth debating whether reclaiming the term could have value for the liberal religious movement.

In the end, the important point is not terminology but the underlying reality the terms point to, namely the variety and the connectedness of various types of liberal theology. Liberal theology is not now—and never has been—monolithic. Yet it retains enough in common that its varied strands, when woven together, generate a richly textured liberal theological fabric.

Basic Characteristics

Four overlapping themes—mediation, flow, autonomy, and ethics— commonly appear in all forms of liberal theology, however else they may differ. They are broad tendencies, not rigid criteria, and in different theologians they will appear in different forms and with different degrees of emphasis. But the presence of these elements is what marks a theological orientation as liberal.

MEDIATION. The central characteristic of liberal theology is mediation, or cultural adaptation. To understand why, we must recognize that liberal theology is a product of the modern world, and more specifically of the Enlightenment. Since liberal theology is commonly understood to have begun with the publication of Schleiermacher's first book, *On Religion: Speeches to Its Cultured Despisers*, in 1799, understanding the task Schleiermacher set for himself in this book will help us see why mediation became the central feature of liberal theology.

While Schleiermacher supported the basic direction of the Enlightenment and borrowed many of its analytical tools, he was concerned that many cultural and intellectual leaders seemed not to appreciate the true value of religion. As he put it, "the life of cultivated persons is removed from everything that would in the least way resemble religion." He addressed the book directly to the intellectuals of his day, the "cultured despisers" of religion, as he called them, in terms that sound remarkably current:

> You have succeeded in making your earthly lives so rich and many-sided that you no longer need the eternal, and after having created a universe for yourselves, you are spared from thinking of that which created you.

Yet rather than dismiss his readers out of hand, Schleiermacher sought to lead them back into the fold by arguing that religion was not to be found in rigid institutional structures or stale theological dogma, as they had supposed, but in an intuition or *feeling* they already had within themselves.

Schleiermacher was trying to mediate between two different ways of looking at the world. He sought to integrate what was of value in both, on several different levels. First, he mediated between philosophy and theology, drawing on the current richness of philosophical thought while retaining his religious commitments. He also mediated between the church and the academy, holding important positions in both of these worlds. Finally, like Beethoven, with whom he was contemporary, Schleiermacher bridged the Enlightenment (classical) and Romantic periods in Western thought. In short, Schleiermacher sought to build a bridge between Christian theology and modern culture.

Mediation has been a central characteristic of liberal theology ever since. As Dorrien explains,

> From the beginning, liberal theology was a third way. It was not radical, infidel, agnostic, or atheist, though it was routinely called all of these; liberal theology was both a morally humanist alternative to Protestant orthodoxy and a religious alternative to rationalistic atheism. It shared the humanistic moral impulses of modern rationalism, ... but it defended biblical religion in a manner that accorded with its image of Christ.

Theologian Paul Lakeland makes the same point in his observation that all modern liberal theologies "are united in their commitment to the mediation of religious thought to a secular world."

For liberals, this mediating approach means that theology needs to be in touch with and respond to the spirit of its own time. Of course, like any other human endeavor, theology reflects the influences of its own social context. But while some theologies have sought to minimize this influence or even to separate from the larger culture, liberalism has embraced it. Among other things, this means that religious ideas are often adapted or restated in terms of the language and values of contemporary culture. It also means that theology often looks to the natural and social sciences, the arts, and other cultural sources in formulating its doctrines and other theological claims. Liberals argue that only in this way can theology remain credible and relevant to the needs of the present. In what could be taken as a prototypical statement of the basic approach of liberal theology, theologian Sallie McFague states,

> As theologians, we should aim for coherence or compatibility between the scientific view and the interpretation of our basic doctrine. That is the bottom line: a theology that avoids this task and settles for an outmoded view is irresponsible and will eventually be seen to be incredible.

Connectedness to the larger culture has characterized American liberal theology from the beginning. To cite one early example, liberal Congregational minister and Bible scholar Joseph Buckminster (1784-1812) was one of the founders of the Boston Athenaeum in 1805. The Athenaeum was dedicated to literary and scientific learning and in effect became Boston's first library and art museum. Buckminster was a leading proponent of the new forms of biblical scholarship that were beginning to emerge from German universities. His essays on biblical criticism appeared alongside essays on literary criticism in the *Monthly Anthology*, the journal published by the Athenaeum's members. In his preaching, Buckminster urged people to "think of the spiritual life in terms of the intellectual life." This message was "based on a tacit agreement among the liberals to equate those realms."

In the late nineteenth century, a different sort of cultural mediation could be seen in the theology of Francis Ellingwood Abbot (1848-1903). Abbot was a cofounder of the Free Religious Association in 1867, a group that broke from the moderate

Unitarians of the time. In his major theological work, *Scientific Theism* (1885), he sought to recast central theological categories in light of new scientific developments, including Darwin's theory of evolution. He argued, for example, that God was not a supernatural being, but rather a force or "infinite intelligibility," an aspect of the universe that forms the basis of moral law and religious virtue. American religious historian Sidney Ahlstrom notes that Abbot was "acclaimed as the first American theologian to develop a system of religious thought in complete consonance with Darwinian evolution." This again is typical of the liberal approach.

In the middle decades of the twentieth century, theologian Henry Nelson Wieman (1884-1975) also developed a naturalistic view of God in line with new scientific and philosophical insights. For Wieman, God was found in the process of "progressive integration" or "creative synthesis" in the universe, a process he eventually came to call "creative interchange." This integrative process was not simply a theoretical construct, nor was it any sort of supernatural or otherworldly reality. Instead, it was a power actually operating in the natural world. Moreover, it was not omnipotent. It created increased value and other forms of human good, but other forces were at work too, including processes of disintegration and destruction. The most thorough development of these ideas can be found in Wieman's most important book, *The Source of Human Good*, published in 1946.

For Wieman, as for Abbot, the idea of God has moved away from the traditional view of an all-powerful supernatural being and toward a naturalistic concept in line with his understanding of contemporary science. While Wieman's particular view, like Abbot's, went further than most theologians of his day were willing to go, both his method and his conclusion are typical of the liberal tendency to turn to cultural sources, including the sciences, in constructive theological work.

The social sciences have also been readily adapted to liberal theology. The social gospel movement is perhaps the most prominent example. This movement held that the Christian gospel was concerned not simply with individual salvation but with social salvation. Christian ideals should be applied to social structures and economic relations, in particular the widespread social unrest in the cities and labor unrest in American industry. Thus, the social gospelers used Christian teachings as the basis for a critique of the existing social order.

The social gospelers also relied heavily on cultural resources. Both their social and theological analyses drew on the methods of the emerging social sciences of the day, especially sociology. And culture was not only the target but the tool of the divine. The goal of the social gospel was nothing less than the establishment of the kingdom of God on earth. Walter Rauschenbusch, the leading theologian of the movement, combined biblical principles and social analysis with the nineteenth century's ideal of progress. For Rauschenbusch, the kingdom of God was "not a concept nor an ideal merely, but an actual historical force... now at work in humanity." It involved "a progressive reign of love in human affairs," which meant that it tended "toward a social order which will best guarantee to all personalities their freest and highest development."

More recently, several liberal theologians are incorporating economic analysis into their work as they reflect theologically on issues such as rampant consumerism, the extreme inequalities of wealth in our society, and the moral and spiritual implications of the global economy. Both Sallie McFague and Douglas Meeks, for example, draw on economic principles as they wrestle with theological questions such as how God is present in the world and how we might think of sin and salvation in a world full of poverty and oppression. At the same time, they use theological insights drawn from their traditions to critique unhealthy economic structures. This methodology reflects the typical liberal adaptation to science and other cultural sources.

FLOW. Several related themes are wrapped up in this second major characteristic of liberal theology. One is that reality involves movement. Whether we are talking about ideas, life situations, society, the natural world, or even the universe, nothing is static. Everything changes over time. Change may not always be smooth or predictable, but it cannot be avoided. Everything is part of a larger dynamic process; nothing is ever finished.

Another theme is interdependence. Liberals tend to emphasize the relational nature of reality. Things flow together in ways that affect each other. This is true of time and history; the past influences the present, and what we do or fail to do in the present affects the future. For liberals, these sorts of influences are open-ended. The past influences the present but does not determine it. This kind of interdependence is part of the reality of nature, culture, and society. The world is an organic whole; nothing can be fully understood or experienced in isolation.

This organic view of reality has been a central feature of liberal theology since the early years of the nineteenth century. Modern Western thought was reacting against the rationality of the Enlightenment, and the movement known as Romanticism was in full flower. If we want to understand how flow and organicism find their way into liberal theology, we must turn to Romanticism.

To begin, the Romantic outlook involves what M. H. Abrams calls a "metaphysics of integration." In this view of the world, things that are divided or opposed to each other will ultimately be reconciled. In Romantic literature, human beings are often depicted as fragmented. They are alienated from themselves or perhaps from others or from nature. From this perspective, the central human task is to seek reintegration. This was true not only of human beings but of the cosmos itself. All things are part of a larger whole, and the direction of the universe is toward some form of final unity.

Another Romantic theme was a tendency to equate nature with the divine, or at least to recognize the divine in nature and to think about both in similar ways. This meant that the distinction between the natural and the supernatural became blurred. By the same token, the distinction between humanity and the rest of the universe was also broken down. Human beings were an integral part of the larger cosmic forces that surrounded them. This view also contributed to the Romantic tendency to see the world as holistic and organic.

We must return to Schleiermacher to understand how these ideas became so important in liberal theology. Schleiermacher's seminal book *On Religion* marks an important point of departure not only for liberal theology but for Romantic thought as well. It would be a mistake to equate early liberal theology with Romanticism, but there are so many overlapping themes that a landmark such as *On Religion* breaks new ground in more than one way. For example, in a move that is critical for both liberal theology and Romantic literature, Schleiermacher completely changed the common understanding of the source of religious knowledge. For thinkers of the Enlightenment, religious knowledge comes from the faculty of human reason. But for Schleiermacher, it comes from a prereflective experience associated with a kind of intuition or "feeling." Human beings need not, indeed *cannot*, reason their way to God. Instead, we are equipped with an innate capacity that Schleiermacher described as a "sense and taste for the infinite" or an "intuition of the universe," to which we merely need open ourselves.

In American liberal theology, these ideas appear with a twist in the work of Ralph Waldo Emerson (1803-1882). Emerson blended the themes of European Romanticism with the New England virtues of individualism and self-reliance. Like the Romantics, he celebrated nature and viewed the universe as a dynamic and organic whole. In his first book, *Nature* (1836), Emerson wrote of a mystical or transcendent unity that has its source in a universal spirit. Humans become conscious of this unity through nature. Emerson urged his readers to abandon their egoism and become "transparent eyeballs" through which the "currents of Universal Being circulate." In this sense, nature is "ever the ally of Religion." For Emerson, God is primarily identified with nature, reflecting the Romantic notion that there is no gap between the finite and the infinite.

While Emerson had an organic worldview that held each individual to be a microcosm of the All, he also endorsed a strong individualism, perhaps expressed most clearly in his dictum "trust thyself" from his essay "Self-Reliance" (1841). Emerson was critical of tradition, which he found stifling to individual freedom: "Whoso would be a man must be a nonconformist." This emphasis on self-reliance provided a rallying cry for American individualism in the nineteenth century. The tension between individualism and organicism, found so clearly in Emerson, has long been a feature of liberal theology.

Developments in the natural sciences during the nineteenth century also contributed to liberal theology's emphasis on flow. The previous two centuries had witnessed astonishing breakthroughs in physics, mathematics, and astronomy. Scientists such as Galileo, Johannes Kepler, and above all Isaac Newton had begun uncovering the natural laws of the universe. Their method involved breaking the world down into its smallest parts in order to study and understand it better. While this approach gave us wonderful new knowledge and made possible many advances in medicine, communications, and other areas, it also produced a sterile and mechanized picture of the universe.

This mechanical view of reality is a large part of what the Romantics, with their holistic and organic worldview, reacted against. The Romantic shift was in line with some important developments in the biological and earth sciences, of which the new concept of evolution was perhaps most significant for theology. While we commonly associate the theory of evolution with Darwin, it made its first important appearance not in biology but in geology. In 1830 a British geologist named Charles Lyell claimed that the earth's present geological form was the product of slow, long-term natural processes. Until this time, the prevailing theory had been catastrophism, which held that the earth was formed through a series of great cataclysmic events, such as the flood depicted in Genesis, and that these events were products of divine intervention. Lyell's theory challenged this view and opened the way for Darwin's theory of natural selection some thirty years later. In a sense, these scientific developments confirmed what the Romantic poets had already insisted upon, namely that the natural world is an organic whole involved in constant change. Metaphors of organism began to replace metaphors of mechanism in our pictures of the world. These nineteenth-century developments in literature, philosophy, and science were to have a profound impact on liberal theology.

Liberalism's emphasis on continuity stood in stark contrast to older orthodox theologies. In the medieval worldview, the world had a fixed hierarchical order. The purpose of nature was to serve humanity, and humanity's purpose was to serve God. Each of these realms was sharply separated from the others. Moreover, the world and its creatures were thought to have been created more or less in their present forms. Even existing social structures and institutions, especially the church, were seen as ordained by God and therefore accepted as normative or simply taken for granted.

This medieval worldview contained clear and rigid categories, which led to strong dualisms, especially between the natural and the supernatural: God is found in the supernatural realm, separate and distant from the natural world. From this vantage point, God acts upon and within the natural world through revelation, miracle, and the incarnation in Christ, but is otherwise removed. This separation was echoed in the sharp distinction drawn between nature and humanity. Other dualisms preserved clear distinctions between the sacred and the secular, good and evil, and those who were saved (the "elect") and those who were not. This basic worldview was incorporated into traditional or orthodox Christian theology well into the eighteenth century and even beyond in some quarters.

In the emerging liberal theology, these once-clear lines became blurred. In line with the new cultural and scientific mindset, liberalism has generally sought to avoid strict dualisms and to emphasize the fundamental continuity of things. Perhaps the most significant theological shift has been the liberal emphasis on God's immanence. As art and science came to see the world as an organic whole and the distinction between the natural and the supernatural dissolved, liberal religious thinkers began to find God in the world rather than removed from it. Emerson's emphasis on the divine in nature, the social gospel emphasis on cultural immanentism, and Wieman's naturalistic theism exemplify this view.

God's immanence continues to be a central feature of liberal theology today. Sallie McFague has developed what she calls an ecological theology, one that emphasizes interdependence and sustainability as central values. For McFague, the old model of a distant God cannot support this view. Instead, she envisions God as deeply present:

> The radical intimacy of God and the world...means that we can experience God's presence anywhere and everywhere. There is no place where God is not.

McFague does not ignore God's transcendent aspect, the beyond-the-world quality that she sees as creating, sustaining, and liberating the world. In this sense, we are radically dependent on a God who is larger than the world. These divine activities are not carried out from a disinterested distance, but rather from an interested and loving involvement. Like many theologians today, McFague stresses both God's radical transcendence and radical immanence.

Theologian Marjorie Hewitt Suchocki, developing themes commonly associated with process theology, stresses the mutuality between God and the world. God's activity influences events in the world and in our lives, but by the same token, the things we do also affect God. In this view, God's power and freedom are shared. As Suchocki puts it,

> God's touch is conditioned by the world, and limited by the world, so that God must ever adapt divine possibilities to the reality of who we are becoming in the total movement of our lives.

[God is] pervasively present, like water, to every nook and cranny of the universe, continuously wooing the universe toward continuous transformation toward its greater good.

This too is an image of God as radically immanent.

Another important dimension of the liberal emphasis on flow is a fluid understanding of religious truth. Traditional Christian theologies understood truth as given once for all time by God or perhaps revealed in Christ or through scripture. In either case, truth once given was complete and unchangeable. This view reflected the older understanding of the world as fixed, an attitude that sought to fit things into static and well-defined categories. There was little awareness of the historical and cultural conditioning of knowledge.

Liberals have rejected this static view and tend to see the world in terms of dynamic elements such as change and growth. This has had an effect on their understanding of truth and meaning. For example, liberal theologians today are likely to say that meaning is constructed rather than given. As theologian Gordon Kaufman explains, "We humans create the structures of meaning within which we come to dwell." By the same token, when liberals use traditional concepts such as revelation, they are likely to say something like "Revelation is continuous." James Luther Adams used this phrase to express the idea that reality is continuously recreated and that as a consequence, no belief system or historical moment may claim any special status: "Meaning has not been finally captured. Nothing is complete, and thus nothing is exempt from criticism." Suchocki also recasts the doctrine of revelation, but in a different way. Using the metaphor of light through a prism, she claims that God "is revealed through the actuality of the world.... [But] the revelation of God is never pure; it is always twofold. God and the world are seen through the same light." Again we see traditional categories reinterpreted from a perspective that emphasizes immanence and mutuality.

For religious liberals, to say that truth is never finally settled is not to say that reality is meaningless or that there are no standards by which to seek and measure truth. It simply recognizes that truth is at least partly a product of our culture and that it will evolve and change over time. We are a long way from the post-modern dilemma of nihilistic relativism, which holds that no standards for discerning truth can be justified.

AUTONOMY. The third central characteristic of liberal theology is autonomy of the self. The self has occupied center stage in Western thought since 1641, the year French philosopher and mathematician René Descartes (1596-1650) concluded that he could be sure of his own existence because he was aware of himself as a thinking being: "I think, therefore I am." Two aspects of Descartes' claim are significant for us. First, it was *thinking*, not feeling or acting, that convinced him. Second, he reached this conclusion *himself*, through his own private reflection, without looking to any external source for validation. He thus came to see himself as a self-authenticating, reasoning individual. This perspective became one of the dominant characteristics of modern thought. And liberal theology, in its eagerness to adapt modern philosophical developments, readily absorbed this idea into its own self-understanding.

The insistence on individual autonomy has shaped liberal religious attitudes and practices in several important ways. It signaled a major shift in the locus of authority. In premodern theology, and still today in many places, authority is located primarily in external sources such as the church or the Bible, even the state. But religious liberals have always mistrusted external authority, believing that nothing can be taken as truth simply because the church or some other established authority says so. Indeed, some liberal groups, such as the Universalists and Freewill Baptists of pre-Revolutionary New England, displayed an almost pathological resistance to institutional authority even within their own movement. This attitude was sometimes referred to as the "right of private judgment."

Suspicion of external authority has meant that the beliefs and practices long ensconced in tradition are subject to challenge and change. Kaufman, for example, expressing the sense of many liberal theologians, insists that "it is impermissible for theologians to take any religious tradition's authoritarian claims...as an unquestioned foundation for theological work." Instead, "theologians today must take full responsibility for all the concepts they use and all the claims they advance." To accept a claim simply because it is part of the tradition would be contrary to the liberal religious mind-set. The larger point is that we religious liberals usually think of ourselves as our own ultimate authority.

The notion of individual autonomy assumes that human beings have a significant degree of freedom, and liberals have always emphasized human freedom. As James Luther Adams put it, "Free choice is a principle without which religion...cannot be liberal." But in this, liberals are not unique. Even traditional orthodox theologies saw human beings as free moral agents, which follows from the belief that God is a free moral agent and that humans are created in God's image. This stance produced a paradox in traditional Christian theology. At one level, humans are absolutely dependent on God for their existence; at another level, they are free and morally responsible beings. The traditional view was that despite (or perhaps because of) their freedom, humans inevitably fall into sin, which means that they are also dependent on God's grace for their salvation. God, not humanity, occupies center stage.

In liberal theology, these roles have been reversed. Liberals in general place less emphasis on human sinfulness, and in contrast to Calvinistic orthodoxy, human nature is understood in mainly positive terms. This means that human beings are far less dependent on God for their fulfillment than in traditional theologies. Indeed, as humans take on more authority for themselves, there is simply less for God to do.

This is not to say that humans are in any sense absolutely free, even in the liberal worldview. Perhaps ironically, as our scientific understanding of the human condition has deepened, liberal theology has tended to diminish the sphere of human freedom.

Adams, for example, recognized that human freedom is contingent; the forms of nature and history "possess a certain given, fateful character." And Kaufman is acutely aware of the constraints imposed on human freedom by biological, historical, sociocultural, and even cosmological conditions. Yet a range of freedom still exists, and it continues to form an important conceptual function in liberal theology. This freedom is now located primarily in our self-consciousness: "Our freedom is at heart an aspect of our human self-reflexiveness: that is, of our having learned to relate" to others and to ourselves, as well as "our having learned to make decisions and take actions" in these relationships. Thus, however radically historical or contingent the human condition is perceived to be, the liberal theological perspective carefully guards against any kind of fatalism or determinism.

ETHICS. American liberal theology in particular has understood itself as an ethical tradition from the beginning. The liberal turn to ethics is often understood as a contrast to the greater emphasis on doctrine found in orthodox theologies. This is basically correct, but the story is more complex. Liberals do not have a monopoly on religious ethics. All theological traditions, including the most conservative orthodoxies, address matters of moral character and social ethics. Yet it remains true that ethics has been a matter of special emphasis in liberal theology, if for no other reason than its own self-understanding.

There are several reasons for the prominence of ethics in liberal religious thought. One is the liberal tendency to see truth as open-ended and changing. As noted earlier, this stance reduces the importance of doctrinal disputes among liberals and leaves more theological energy for other matters, including ethics. Another factor can be traced to a major conceptual move by the great German philosopher Immanuel Kant (1724-1804) in the late eighteenth century. Kant shifted the grounding of human religiousness from the realm of scientific or "theoretical" reason, where it had been located by earlier modern philosophers, into the realm of what he called moral or practical reason. This shift is an important part of the philosophical underpinnings of liberal theology.

Perhaps the most important factor in the liberal emphasis on ethics arose ironically out of a dispute over doctrine. The doctrine in question was the proper understanding of human nature, and the dispute was a key part of a general liberal critique of Calvinist orthodoxy. This disagreement began in the late eighteenth century and extended well into the nineteenth.

At least since the early seventeenth century, one of Calvinism's central doctrines was the "total depravity of the self." In North America, this doctrine especially characterized the religious out-look of the New England Puritans, but it was widespread among all groups in the Reformed (Calvinist) church tradition. Total depravity was rooted in the doctrine of original sin, meaning that human beings were utterly lacking in any capacity to save themselves. This belief was linked to the doctrine of election, which held that only a select few would be saved and that God had already chosen them. The result was a dreary view of the human condition that left little room for hope. In fact, it seemed to offer no reason for good behavior, since there was nothing one could do to earn salvation. And if you were already chosen, there was nothing you could do to lose it.

In fact, even the strictest Calvinist theology offered a basis for ethics. It revolved around the general belief that those who were chosen to be saved would tend naturally toward morally upstanding and pious lives. And since most people wanted to think of themselves as among the elect, there was a certain encouragement to the kinds of good behavior that would justify their hope. But no one could ever be sure, and the overall cast of the doctrine of human depravity remained gloomy. Pious behavior was often as much the result of fear as of faith.

Liberal theology challenged all this by offering a radically different understanding of human nature. Where the Calvinists dwelt on the negative aspects of the human condition, the liberals stressed the positive. This difference was linked to a very different understanding of the nature of God. If the Calvinist God was a distant and stern sovereign, the liberal God was a loving and benevolent father figure. And because humans are made in God's image, they are essentially good in their core being. The phrase "likeness to God" came to represent the early liberal view of human nature. The liberal Congregational minister Charles Chauncy used this phrase as early as 1785. Half a century later, in 1828, Unitarian minister William Ellery Channing preached a well-known sermon using "Likeness to God" as his title. Stating a widely held liberal view, Channing claimed that "the Divinity within us...makes us more and more partakers of the moral perfection of the Supreme Being."

This elevated view of human nature emphasized ethics in several ways. First, there was the liberal doctrine of human freedom, which was defined in opposition to Calvinism. The liberals saw Calvinism as a deterministic system in which the self had no power or freedom. This was an exaggeration of the Calvinist view, but it allowed them to claim that liberal theology empowered the self by affirming free will. The liberal insistence on autonomy meant that individuals could determine for themselves what was good, and this in turn implied an ethical obligation to create the good they envisioned.

A more important factor was what came to be called the moral argument against Calvinism. Channing wrote an essay with this very title in 1820. Just the year before, he had preached what was to become his most famous sermon, "Unitarian Christianity," in which he launched a sharp attack on what he saw as the moral failure of Calvinism:

> It tends to discourage the timid, to give excuses to the bad, to feed the vanity of the fanatical, and to offer shelter to the bad feelings of the malignant. By shocking, as it does, the fundamental principles of morality, and by exhibiting a severe and partial Deity, it tends strongly to pervert the moral faculty, to form a gloomy, forbidding, and servile religion, and to lead men to substitute censoriousness, bitterness, and persecution, for a tender and impartial charity.

He then offered the liberal view as a corrective:

> We believe that all virtue has its foundation in the moral na-
> ture of man, that is, in conscience, or his sense of duty, and
> in the power of forming his temper and life according to
> conscience. We believe that these moral faculties are the
> grounds of responsibility, and the highest distinctions of
> human nature, and that no act is praiseworthy, any farther
> than it springs from their exertion.

In these and other public challenges to Calvinist orthodoxy, liberal
theology named itself as an ethical theology.

This positive view of human nature also led liberals to believe
that the role of theology was not simply to articulate doctrine but
to contribute to character formation and the development of the
human potential for goodness. Religion became a means for what
was called self-culture or self-improvement. Manuals such as
Unitarian minister Henry Ware Jr.'s *On the Formation of Christian
Character* (1831) and Congregational minister Horace Bushnell's
Christian Nurture (1847) began to appear, setting the tone for liberal theology throughout the nineteenth century.

In addition to its early emphasis on personal morality, liberal
theology also stressed social ethics. From the beginning, liberal
theology understood itself at least partly in prophetic terms, as offering a critique of the larger culture. Liberals have always been
among those who called society to account in the face of injustice,
often stressing the need for social reform. This was a natural outgrowth of the liberal belief in human potential and the commitment to human betterment. An early example is Unitarian
minister Joseph Tuckerman, who helped redefine the role of ministry during the 1820s and 1830s through his work as a "minister-
at-large" serving the urban poor in Boston. Social ministry has
been part of the liberal tradition ever since.

Toward the end of the nineteenth century, the liberal social
impulse came to the surface in the social gospel movement.
Dorrien claims that this was "the first Christian movement in the

history of Christianity to imagine the progressive transformation of society." The social gospel was prompted in large part by a perceived need to respond to several serious social crises, including widespread labor conflict and urban unrest. Theologically, the movement was grounded in the teachings of Jesus, which were now interpreted as social teachings and applied to the social issues of the day. The liberal theological perspective called for a better society, and the liberal Protestant churches were eager to help create it. They sought a new social spirit based on Christian love and supported economic reforms such as profit sharing and regulation of child labor. Some liberal clergy got involved in the labor movement, urban political reform, or social projects such as Hull House in Chicago. But while its contributions to theology and to social change were significant, the social gospel was basically a middle-class movement. It retained the liberal emphasis on gradual reform and for the most part stopped short of advocating any radical social change.

Liberal theology's emphasis on social ethics continued into the twentieth century, but the social conditions changed, requiring theological adjustments. Liberalism's optimistic assessment of human nature and social progress had been seriously challenged by World War I and subsequent events, including the Great Depression and the rise of fascism in Europe. A new group of theologians, led by Reinhold Niebuhr (1892-1971) in the United States, undertook a sustained theological critique of liberalism. Among other things, Niebuhr complained of liberal weaknesses in social ethics. James Luther Adams took these critiques seriously and sought to revitalize liberal theological ethics during the middle decades of the twentieth century.

Like the liberal theologians of the past, Adams focused on human nature, but he was less sanguine than his nineteenth-century predecessors. Adams saw the human condition as tragic. By this he meant that human beings were capable of creating both great good and great evil and that the same human creative powers were at work in either case. Adams understood social ethics in terms of power, and he linked power to both God and human beings. He expressed these themes in an important essay written in 1950, entitled "Theological Bases of Social Action":

> The decisive element in social action is the exercise of power, and the character of social action is determined by the character of the power expressed. Power always has a double character: first, as the expression of God's law and love; second, as the exercise of human freedom.... The expression of power in the dimensions of both freedom and necessity at its most profound levels must be understood religiously, that is, in terms of its theological bases.

Through the proper exercise of power, humans are capable of moral and social progress, as early liberal theology taught, but they need to commit to it rather than simply trusting to a form of natural progress. More than this, they need to create and nurture social institutions or voluntary associations through which this work can be focused and sustained.

> The voluntary association...offers the means of breaking through old social structures in order to meet new needs. It is a means of dispersing power, in the sense that power is the capacity to participate in making social decisions....In short, the voluntary association is a means for the institutionalizing of gradual revolution.

Adams's writings on voluntary associations are widely regarded as a major contribution to twentieth-century theological ethics.

A prominent example of the ethical emphasis in contemporary liberal theology is the work of theological ethicist James Gustafson, who shifts the focus away from humanity, where liberal theology had long placed it, and toward God. Yet Gustafson's view of God is very different from that found in traditional Christian theology. Like many liberal theologians, he believes that God must be conceived in ways that are consistent with contemporary science, ruling out any concept of God that involves divine moral agency or will. Indeed, this approach rules out anthropomorphic images altogether. Here Gustafson is in agreement with liberal theologians such as Gordon Kaufman and Sallie McFague. God, then, comes to symbolize "the ultimate ordering power of the universe" that enables life to be ordered in a way that enhances the well-being of all things. The human ethical obligation is to live in ways that recognize and nurture the relationship of each individual to the whole and to God.

A different ethical perspective is found in the work of Unitarian Universalist ethicist Sharon Welch. Like other liberals, Welch rejects what she calls "the god of classical theism." But unlike most others, she doesn't bother to reconceptualize God in scientific terms or otherwise seek to rehabilitate God as a central symbol. Instead, she emphasizes divinity, not as a shorthand for a particular quality of the universe but as "a quality of relationships, lives, events, and natural processes...that provide orientation, focus, and guidance for our lives." Welch calls for an "ethic of risk," one that recognizes that "we cannot guarantee decisive change in the near future or even in our lifetime," but also knows that we must continue the "long struggle for justice" in any case. Welch has clearly moved away from the traditional liberal optimism, yet her writing continues to express a strong sense of hope and joy. In her more recent work, Welch argues explicitly for a humanist approach to ethics and appears to no longer think of herself as a theologian. Yet her work can be understood as part of the tradition of liberal-progressive theology that has long emphasized social ethics.

These four themes—mediation, flow, autonomy, and ethics—have been central identifying features of liberal theology from the beginning. But there is more to liberal theology than these "markers." A deeper appreciation requires an understanding of liberal theology philosophical and social sources. In the next chapter, we will turn to this task.

Sources of Liberal Theology
in the Modern Period

THE STORY OF LIBERAL THEOLOGY is a modern story. In casual conversation, we use the word *modern* to mean "up to date" or "current." But in historical and philosophical writing, *modern* is a technical term referring to a specific period in Western culture. When we say that liberal theology is a child of modernity, we are saying that it has been shaped by modernity's characteristics.

Although scholars hold varying views about when the modern period began, most agree that it appeared with the emergence of modern science and modern philosophy in the sixteenth and seventeenth centuries. In science, the key figure is Galileo Galilei (1564-1642), and the key development was a new form of scientific method. Galileo combined theory with observation and experiment in new ways. In earlier periods, science was linked to metaphysics, so that scientists typically inquired into the ultimate purposes served by the objects of their investigations. Like theologians and philosophers, they speculated about the deeper meaning or essence of things. Galileo shifted the emphasis from the metaphysical to the physical and in the process reduced the scope of the questions scientists asked. Rather than look for some ultimate meaning, he was interested in "expressing the laws of nature as mathematical relationships among measurable variables." In other words,

> Galileo asked not why objects move, but how they move. He was content to describe how phenomena progress, and he completely ignored questions about the purposes they serve, which he saw as irrelevant to the problems in which he was interested.

This shift in method became a central feature of modern thought.

In philosophy the work of René Descartes (1596-1650) marked the beginning of the modern era. For our purposes, the most important aspect of Descartes' thought was his absolute separation of mind and matter. His starting point was radical doubt. Descartes was searching for a sure foundation for knowledge, something he could believe with absolute certainty. He found that he could doubt what his senses seemed to tell him, and therefore could doubt the existence of the physical world and even of his own body. But all of this doubt made him aware of himself as a thinking-doubting being. The one thing he could be absolutely sure of was his own existence: "I think, therefore I am," as he famously expressed it.

But how can one doubt his body and yet be sure of his own existence? Descartes' assumption led him to the unfortunate conclusion that we human beings are, in our most essential cores, simply abstract or disembodied subjects. Our physical bodies are merely external contingencies, accidents of form. What counts is the mind, or consciousness. Descartes' conclusion became the new starting point for philosophical reflection, and his mind-body dualism became a central feature of the modern way of thinking. More importantly for us, it also found its way into modern liberal religious thought and continues to plague us today.

The modern period reached its peak in the Enlightenment, a broad cultural and intellectual movement extending roughly from the late seventeenth to the late eighteenth centuries. Its centers of gravity were Germany, France, and Britain, but its influences were felt throughout Western Europe and North America. Enlightenment thinking affected nearly every area of public life, including the sciences, law, politics and government, the arts, philosophy, and religion. Such new ideas as democracy, individual rights, equality, nationalism, and capitalism began to emerge and had a profound effect on existing social and political structures. Some historians see the modern period as marking a basic shift from an aristocratic to a democratic society. This shift was encouraged by the explosion of new scientific discoveries and by the increasing commercial and urban population that sought to apply this new knowledge to practical uses in industry, transportation, and other fields.

As modernity became more engrained, people began to think of themselves and their own time as fundamentally different from earlier periods. They felt they were involved in something historically new. Contemporary German philosopher Jürgen Habermas agrees. For Habermas, the central characteristic of modernity is the development of a historical consciousness. In other words, modernity consciously sets itself apart from earlier historical periods. The norms of the past no longer apply. Modern thought looks only to itself for its justification. Unlike the past when external and traditional authorities could be relied on, in modernity "the self-defining subject must seek moral guidance from within." For the modern human being, thought and action become self-authenticating. This represents an enormous change, one that has profound implications for religion and theology.

Scholarly debate about modernity and its consequences has raged for at least two centuries. While much is still disputed, there is much we can agree on, especially if we focus on the aspects of modernity that are directly linked to liberal theology.

It may be helpful to distinguish between two types of discussions about modernity. The first is the "philosophical discourse of modernity," to use Habermas's term. This approach focuses on the key philosophical ideas that emerged during modernity and helped define its basic character. The second relates to modernity's social conditions, which focus on the social institutions, economic structures, and other material conditions of life in the modern period. The relationship between modernity and liberal theology is often explored only through philosophical discussion. But even theologians are affected by the social structures they inhabit and the social changes going on around them. This is especially true for liberals, since one of liberal theology's most defining characteristics is a proclivity for adapting itself to its own cultural conditions. This means we must examine both modernity's ideas and the social contexts and implications of these ideas if we truly want to understand the ways modernity has influenced liberal theology.

Philosophical Themes

Despite the variety of perspectives on modernity, there is widespread agreement about its central philosophical themes. These themes overlap considerably, and naming them is in some ways arbitrary. Different scholars may use different categories, but most agree on the basic points. It is helpful to think of six interrelated themes: subjectivity, reason, progress, universality, criticism, and method.

SUBJECTIVITY. It has become common to say that modern Western philosophy is marked by a "turn to the subject." This "turn" begins with Descartes' affirmation of himself as a thinking being. It radically changed the way we look at the world by placing the self at the center and defining everything else in relation to it.

As significant as Descartes' move was, the process of elevating human subjectivity actually began a century earlier, during the Protestant Reformation. The Reformation was a complex movement involving many issues, but at its heart it challenged the authority of the church. Of course the churches that emerged out of the main branch of the Reformation reestablished church authority in new forms, but the fundamental principle of protest, from which the term *Protestant* derives, remained. Church authority was no longer taken for granted. As Habermas puts it, "Against faith in the authority of preaching and tradition, Protestantism asserted the authority of the subject relying upon his own insight."

We may say, then, that the turn to subjectivity represents in part a rejection of external authority. Nearly a century ago, the great liberal Protestant theologian Ernst Troeltsch (1865-1923) argued that independence from external authority, especially the church, was modernity's central characteristic. In his analysis, Troeltsch contrasted modern civilization with what he called the "Church-civilization" of premodern periods. The era of Church-civilization was "above all things a *civilization of authority*." Both secular and religious authority were centralized in the Church. As external authority waned, other forms of authority were sought in its place. In modernity, this new authority became the individual human being. This shift received its highest expression during the Enlightenment, especially in the philosophy of Immanuel Kant, whose injunction "Have the courage to use your own reason" became a motto of the Enlightenment perspective. The emphasis on the authority of the individual eventually manifested itself in new conceptions of law and civil government that recognized individual rights as a restraint on state power and authority. Subjectivity thus carries with it an important dimension of individualism and autonomy of action.

But subjectivity is more than just a principle of autonomy; it also affects the nature and form of every dimension of modern culture. In science, for example, the knowing individual is elevated, while nature is disenchanted and objectified. In morality, the person is free to determine his or her own course of right action and to understand that course as valid precisely because it is self-determined. In art, both form and content are determined by inward reflection and expressive self-realization. In government, democracy becomes the political expression of the modern spirit because of its protection in principle of the individual against state authority. By the same token, capitalism becomes modernity's characteristic economic form because it allows the individual the widest possible range of economic expression, free in principle from state interference. Thus in every dimension of public and private life, modernity signals a major shift away from all forms of external authority and moves toward the internal authority of the autonomous individual.

REASON. Modernity celebrated human reason. In the psychology of the early modern period, reason was seen as a distinct faculty of the human mind. This faculty made it possible for humans to formulate ideas clearly, as well as to examine and solve problems. Because of the shift from external to internal authority, humans felt free to investigate the entire world without worrying whether their findings were in line with church doctrine or other established authority. We can see here how the elevation of reason is connected to the emergence of subjectivity. Habermas emphasizes this by using terms such as "subjective reason" or "subject-centered rationality" when referring to this aspect of modernity. The point is that human reason became the final judge of all things, not only in science but also in the process of deciding philosophical and religious truth.

Modern rationality is individualistic and will-based. As rational beings, we are endowed with a disposition to acquire knowledge. But we seek more than knowledge. Reason also allows us to fulfill intentions, formulate goals, and take actions calculated to meet them. Habermas described this as a "purposive rationality, which is tailored to the cognitive-instrumental dimension." What he meant is that from the perspective of modernity, the reasoning individual wants not only to know but to master its external reality. One consequence is that the subject ends up becoming separated from the world, which is seen as an object to be observed, studied, and mastered. This separation is in part a consequence of Descartes' mind-body split.

The modern emphasis on the reasoning person helped shape a new understanding of the world. When modern subjects looked at the world, they saw order. They saw phenomena that obey natural laws, laws that could be discovered and understood by means of this same faculty of reason. All this confidence in reason was justified by the advances made in the natural sciences during this period, especially in physics and mathematics. This process eventually led to deeper scrutiny of social and political institutions and contributed to the conditions that helped bring about such major social upheavals as the French and American revolutions.

PROGRESS. A third central characteristic of the modern spirit is what Troeltsch called "its self-confident optimism and belief in progress." Philosopher and religious scholar Cornel West refers to this as a "belief in the unlimited possibilities of individuals in society when guided by reason." For Troeltsch, this sense of confidence was a key aspect of the struggle for freedom during the Enlightenment. It also had an important effect on many traditional theological concepts. For example, doctrines such as original sin, which left human beings incapable of redeeming themselves, gave way to a sense of continuing development and upward progress "to unknown heights."

English sociologist David Lyon echoes this idea by suggesting that modernity reflects an "unprecedented dynamism," a "forward looking thrust [that] relates strongly to belief in progress and the power of human reason to produce freedom." During the early modern period, advances in the sciences, new ideas about law and government, and other developments produced a general sense that anything was possible. The future was unlimited. People began to think of history as having a direction toward ever-increasing progress.

Progress took on a new energy in the nineteenth century, when it seemed to be validated by the principle of evolution as it was emerging in sciences such as geology and biology. Evolution also contributed to the belief in social progress and the possibility of human improvement which characterized the liberal religious outlook during this period and came to be reflected in liberal theology. One of the most interesting expressions of this belief was Unitarian minister and social reformer James Freeman Clarke's (1810-1888) theological affirmation of "the progress of mankind onward and upward forever."

The belief in progress also had a negative side. When combined with the biblical notion of a chosen people, it led to the idea of manifest destiny, through which European American Protestants came to think of themselves as God's new chosen people. The racism inherent in this concept is surely one of modernity's most troubling legacies, and it is important to see how these ideas emerged from the larger modern belief in progress.

UNIVERSALITY. In modernity, people came to believe that certain ideas or traits are universally true, shared throughout the world by all people and all cultures. While our postmodern situation has made us more attuned to difference, the concept of universality is engrained in us. For example, we are used to thinking that the world is governed by a set of universal laws—gravity, the laws of motion, the properties of light. These do not operate one way in North America and another in Japan or even Mars. By the same token, we hear things like "People share a common human nature" and "At bottom all people are alike" or find ourselves saying, "All religions at their cores are basically the same" (religious liberals especially tend to make this particular claim). These ideas are so common that it is easy to forget they are products of modernity.

One of the most interesting episodes of the modern tendency to universalize involves an eighteenth-century movement known as *natural theology*, or *deism*. This was the first European theological movement to understand religion as a global or universal phenomenon and it is an important part of the historical background for liberal theology.

Of course, the deists were not the first Europeans to be aware that other cultures had religious traditions. Nearly three centuries of European conquest and colonization, not to mention the Crusades and other religious wars dating back several centuries more, had at least exposed European Christians to other religions. But the deist view was different. Its followers believed that truths about God and other religious matters could be discovered through human reason, unaided by divine revelation. They also claimed that this reason-based "natural" religion was the true form of religion. Religions grounded in revelation, along with the "primitive" religions of other cultures, were regarded as false or inferior. This was an astonishingly arrogant claim, especially since most of these thinkers had little or no knowledge about other traditions. Yet their claim made sense within the Enlightenment worldview, and it generated a line of modern religious thought that has become ingrained in liberal theology.

The deists believed that all human beings had an innate human religious sense that was the basis of all "true" religion. It may take different forms in different cultures, but the central truths it affirmed would be the same because these truths were reached through reason, itself a universal trait. In other words, any reasoning individual who explored this religious sense would eventually arrive at the same conclusions. This approach led to a fairly sterile view of religion, one that devalued peoples' particular beliefs and practices.

The significant point for modern liberalism is that in the deist view, all historical religions are seen as particular instances of the general phenomenon of human religiousness. This relativizes Christianity, making it just one of many forms of religious expression. It also challenges claims of Christian uniqueness, and carried to its logical conclusion, removes God from any involvement in history. God's will is basically equated with the laws of nature, and both can be discerned through reason. This perspective accounts in part for the common and overly simplistic image of deism as affirming a kind of "clockmaker" God, who sets things in motion, establishes regular laws to govern them, and then gets out of the picture. In fact, reliance on unaided reason and an insistence on making universal claims are the central characteristics of deism.

Today we are aware of the many problems created when we are too quick to make universal claims. A tendency to see things as basically the same can easily blind us to the richness of the diversity among us. It can also make us overlook circumstances that call for different responses in particular cases. British scientist and philosopher Stephen Toulmin emphasizes this point when he suggests that modernity tends to frame all questions in terms that are independent of context. At its worst, this approach can lead to forms of cultural imperialism. Yet the modern notion of universality has also made it possible for us to develop principles such as universal human rights and equality before the law. This ambiguity is present in many features of modernity, just as it is in liberal theology.

CRITICISM. The modern mind-set includes a conviction that everything must be subject to criticism. This is not just an attitude; it is a philosophical principle of free critical inquiry. As Kant put it, "Our age is, in especial degree, the age of criticism, and to criticism everything must submit." In modernity, this principle merges with the emphasis on the self, and contributes to the notion that all claims of external authority, including especially the state and the church, are subject to challenge. It also calls for internal self-examination: Even reason itself is subject to criticism. This critical mind-set culminated in Immanuel Kant, who, we might say, formalized criticism into *critique.*

Scholar and philosopher Charlene Spretnak, in her otherwise negative treatment of modernity, holds up the principle of free inquiry as modernity's "one profoundly corrective element, one grandly idealistic value, which eventually exposed the false claims and partial truths of its own dogma." In other words, criticism becomes a kind of self-redeeming corrective principle. As we will see, this principle eventually led to the questioning of many features of the very system that produced it. Sociologist David Lyon sees a paradox here:

> Although the Enlightenment and thus the modern project were designed to eliminate uncertainty and ambivalence, autonomous reason would always have its doubts. It was bound to if it wished to avoid relapsing into "dogma." Relativism of knowledge was built into modern thought.

This critical attitude supported both the constant challenge to external authority and the constant reevaluation of one's own claims. These methods or processes, in turn, became important characteristics of liberal theology.

METHOD. Before the modern period, science and philosophy had been largely deductive, with analysis moving from the general to the particular. Philosophers typically started with an accepted principle or proposition and sought to extrapolate other conclusions from it or to apply it in particular cases. We still use this form of reasoning in many situations today. But the modern period witnessed a trend toward inductive analysis, which involved moving from the particular to the general. Bits of data, experiences, and beliefs were catalogued and examined for their common features. The central task of reasoned analysis was unification. To *know* something meant to place all its parts in correct relationship to each other. This new approach to reasoning also means that modern knowledge is reductive; it reduces things to their lowest common denominator, often disregarding differences as irrelevant. In other words, modern knowledge moves from the complex to the simple, from apparent diversity to underlying unity. This new approach also contributed to modernity's emphasis on universality.

The modern approach is not just about new methods but about a new attitude toward inquiry itself. In many ways, the process of inquiry was thought to be as important as the outcome or content it produced. Human reason might not be able to know or discover everything, but it could ask the right questions. And by applying the proper methods of reasoned inquiry, it could make progress in knowledge and understanding. Yet progress in this context did not mean simply an increase in the quantity of our knowledge. People began to ask such questions as, "How do we know what we know? What does it mean to know something?" In other words, the modern period, and especially the Enlightenment, sought greater understanding of the nature of knowledge itself.

Social Characteristics

Modernity involves not only a philosophical discourse, but social and material characteristics that set it apart from previous historical periods. Commentators disagree on which of modernity's social conditions are most significant. Ernst Troeltsch, for example, was concerned with a large range of social issues, including the formation of militaristic nation states, the emergence of capitalism, the growth of applied science and technology, the effects of population increase, and the rise of the middle class, to name a few. David Lyon, in turn, emphasizes capitalism, new forms of social differentiation, the urbanization of society, and the spread of means-end calculation to all areas of life. Three of these features—capitalism, differentiation, and rationalization—are especially relevant to our understanding of liberal theology, and discussing them here will help later when we look at the challenges to liberal theology arising out of postmodernity.

CAPITALISM. Just as democracy is modernity's natural political form, so capitalism is its characteristic economic expression. Lyon describes capitalism as "the most conspicuous motor driving" the modern social world. And in an insightful essay written in 1907, Troeltsch notes,

> The essence of capitalism is that the means of production (soil, machinery, or money) are geared to produce the maximum amount of goods at the maximum rate of turnover for a free and anonymous market.... This huge, all-consuming giant works with the property of unknown owners, for unknown buyers, motivated only by the calculation of profit and favorable sales opportunities.

Capitalism's basic features include the pursuit of profit, a constant need for new sources of raw material and labor, and unlimited accumulation of capital in private hands. Materially, it has dramatically raised overall standards of living, created the economic basis for the rise of the middle and professional classes, and generated what Troeltsch called a "shower of gold" for a few, while relegating many to society's economic margins.

One of the social consequences of capitalism is that it locates production largely in urban centers, which creates a massive population shift as people move in large numbers from rural to urban areas. The result is that traditional social structures break down and traditional methods of production are eroded. The modern principle of individual autonomy leads to free and unregulated markets, and competitive pressure increases. This in turn produces pressure for what David West describes as "greater productive efficiency and accelerating rates of economic growth."

For Troeltsch, capitalism's moral and spiritual consequences were as important as its social consequences. First, a greatly increased economic ambition leads to "a growing delight in comfort and luxury, a colossal practical materialism." In addition, economic principles are applied to every facet of our lives, so that our whole existence is increasingly calculated and measured. Capitalism's most telling effect, however, "is an abstract, depersonalizing rationalism." Producers are driven by growth and profits, while the ultimate consumers remain anonymous. And modern modes of thought, which tend to break things down to their smallest parts, lead to such modern methods of production as "the infinite division of labor, which destroys the worker's sense of personal involvement with his product." All of these effects are logical outgrowths of the main features of modernity, including autonomy of the self and the use of universal reason. In other words, the logic of capitalism reflects the logic of modernity.

DIFFERENTIATION. The modern methods of inquiry that reduced wholes to their smallest parts were not limited to science and philosophy nor even to industrial production. They were also applied to social structures. The modern way of looking at the world generated a process of social differentiation, which led to the division of life into separate spheres. Work life was separated from home life and from leisure; religion was separated from politics and other forms of public life. This process was linked to the increasing secularization of society as a whole, as well as to the emergence of a professional class. "Tasks once performed by the family or the Church were taken over by schools, youth cultures, and the mass media on the one hand, or by local hospitals and welfare departments on the other." Social differentiation is also related to modernity's emphasis on the subject. Jürgen Habermas refers to it as a process of *disremption*, in which spheres of knowledge are separated from each other as well as from spheres of belief and from everyday life. As a result, "religious life, state, and society as well as science, morality, and art are transformed into just so many embodiments of the principle of subjectivity."

The process of differentiation had important consequences for religion. As faith was separated from knowledge and religion from politics, the sphere of religion was constricted. The result was that religion was no longer able to function as a unifying moral and cultural force. Ironically, while the new self-conscious and rational subjectivity was strong enough to undermine religion, it was not strong enough to create a new unifying power in its place. In the famous dictum of German philosopher Georg Hegel (1770-1831), the finite subject was asked to shoulder an infinite task, an effort that was doomed from the start. The disremption is permanent; self-authentication becomes self-alienation. The result is that "modernity has bequeathed to us a world split into social segments each governed by its own rules, implicit and explicit."

RATIONALIZATION. German sociologist Max Weber (1864-1920) used the term *rationalization* a century ago to describe the process that happens as modern forms of reason are extended to social, political, and economic life. In this context, rationalization involves not simply the use of reason but of a particular form of reasoning devoted to rigorous means-end calculation. This is sometimes described as *purposive* or *instrumental* rationalization.

Lyon notes that this rationalizing process led to "the gradual adopting of a calculating attitude towards more and more aspects of life." And as reliance on efficient calculation increased, the place of traditional values, even morality itself, decreased. We might say that morality was redefined to place higher value on efficiency than, say, community or relationship or happiness. Thus, law was freed from religion and formalized into a system of rules that could be calculated and efficiently administered. Government became "a more systematically organized administration or 'bureaucracy' [in which] decisions are made according to fixed and predictable rules rather than at the discretion of trusted individuals." As Weber sees it, even art and music were rationalized, art through the "rational utilization of lines and spatial perspectives" and music by rationally worked-out structures and harmonies.

The most fully rationalized area has been economics. As noted, capitalism as a form of economic organization encourages (demands, really) rational calculation. The impetus for greater efficiency is built in. Everything is calculated, from initial investment, to labor and other expenses of production, to profit and loss. As Weber puts it, "So far as the transactions are rational, calculation underlies every single action."

Perhaps even more significant than rationalization's social or structural effects are what we might call its psychic effects. By the time of the Enlightenment, Western culture had come to think of itself as modern. This quickly led to "a strong, though not uncontested, belief in the superiority of its own thought, institutions and values." Rationalization was the key factor in this belief— Western culture was more modern precisely because it was more rational, and more rational meant superior. As Australian political theorist David West notes,

> The West claims henceforth that its institutions and thought
> bear a privileged relation to a uniquely valid rationality....
> Europeans come to see themselves as more modern, more
> advanced or more developed than peoples they now describe
> as traditional, backward or primitive—and whom they
> sometimes even see as being incapable of such development.

Ironically, while reason was conceived in modernity as a feature of the autonomous individual, rationalization has led to the
loss of much autonomy. In its unceasing calculations in search of
greater efficiency, rationalization also produces a need for control,
which is often at odds with autonomy. Finally, as anyone who has
ever worked on a factory production line knows, efficient and rational systems also reduce their human participants to interchangeable parts. As Lyon observes, "Supposedly autonomous
individuals, liberated from the authorities of tradition to forge
their own destiny, find themselves mocked by the machine-like
systems they now inhabit."

Some of the links between modernity and liberal theology are
obvious, such as the strong emphasis on individual autonomy in
both. Other connections have been implied, such as liberal theology's mistrust of traditional authority and its tendency to turn to
the sciences. But much of the story remains to be told. In order to
deepen our understanding of modernity's influence, we will trace
two sets of modern philosophical influences on liberal theology:
rational religion and Scottish commonsense philosophy.

Rational Religion

A strand of religious and philosophical thought known as rational
religion emerged out of a debate that took place during the
Enlightenment around the grounding of religious knowledge. The
debate was about whether the true source of religious knowledge
was divine revelation or human reason. Three overlapping stages
in the development of this line of thought include an expansion of
the claims made on behalf of reason, a refinement of the nature of
reason, and a move away from reason toward experience as the
proper source of human religious knowledge.

While the general direction of this development is fairly clear, its
movement is not always linear. The arrival of each new stage did not
mean that the emphases of the prior stages disappeared. Revelation,
for example, despite the best efforts of the Enlightenment, contin-

ues today as one of the central categories of Christian theology, even for some liberals. And reason continues to hold an important place in liberal theology even after it seemed to be displaced by experience. Indeed, since the early nineteenth century, liberals have in many ways simply recast the old reason-revelation debate into a reason-experience debate, and we seem to go through cycles with one or the other in favor. Despite these ambiguities, we can trace a fairly clear trajectory.

The doctrine of revelation is classically defined as God's self-disclosure to human beings. There are many different understandings of when and how this happens. Nearly all forms of Christian theology stress God's revelation through the coming of Jesus, usually described in terms of incarnation. Revelation is thought to take place in other ways as well, such as through scripture understood as God's word, through some form of personal experience, or even through the natural world. Whatever the means of revelation, two points are fundamental: First, we never know all of God because much is hidden in ultimate mystery; and second, our knowledge of God is always the result of God's move, not ours. It is a grace we may receive if we are open to it, but we can't achieve it ourselves.

As modernity progressed, the new emphasis on the powers of human reason eventually challenged revelation as the sole source of religious knowledge. English philosopher John Locke (1632-1704) is a central figure in the first stage of this challenge. Locke distinguished knowledge from belief. Knowledge starts with perception of the world through our senses. Reason allows us to make deductions and draw inferences from our perceptions and extends our knowledge. When we accept propositions we arrived at by means of these deductions, we may say that we have "knowledge" of them.

Unlike knowledge, belief involves accepting something as true without direct observation or reasoned deduction. We may, for example, accept something as true simply because someone in authority told us it is true. For Locke, as for other modern thinkers, this would not be an adequate basis for belief. On the other hand, if the source is someone whose knowledge we trust, we may accept it as true based on what Locke calls "the credit of the proposer." In fact, we believe many things this way, since in our daily lives we normally don't have the time or the resources for carrying out independent investigations of everything.

On the question of religious knowledge, Locke combined reason and revelation. He began with reason, holding that reason can provide us with knowledge of God. In other words, it was possible to make a convincing rational case for God's existence. Locke also believed that God made revelations to human beings and that many of these involved matters beyond our actual knowledge. But we are nevertheless entitled to assent to their truth because of the high "credit" of God as their proposer. Locke also applied this principle to the teachings of Jesus, which we may accept as revealed truths.

For Locke, reason and revelation overlap to some extent, and some truths may be discoverable by either means. But Locke claimed that we hold truths discovered through reason with more certainty, assuming a kind of priority over revelation. We also cannot accept a proposition received by revelation if it contradicts our reason. It is pointless to try to accept such things on faith, since "faith can never convince us of anything that contradicts our knowledge." The proper sphere of faith concerns matters "above reason," things that do not contradict reason yet remain beyond its reach. But even here, reason acts as the final judge once such matters are presented to us. In other words, the truth of revelation is subject to confirmation by reason. Locke significantly reduced the role of divine revelation in religious knowledge.

It is a fairly short step from Locke to the deists, who dispensed with revelation altogether. They held that all of the central truths of religion, including knowledge of God, could be derived from reason alone. In addition to knowledge of God, some deists developed a program of specific religious truths derived through reason. These included the duty to worship God, the importance of virtue and piety, the need to repent our shortcomings, and the reality of reward and punishment in an afterlife. More than this, they held these "truths" to be universal. In other words, these were not just the beliefs of this particular group; they could be affirmed by any rational being.

From our perspective, this grand claim was chauvinistic and overblown, to say the least. On closer analysis, the deists' universal truths basically constituted a generic form of Christianity, with specific claims about Jesus removed. They pushed the claims of reason so far that even other Enlightenment philosophers began to balk, leading to what may be called the careful refinement of reason.

Scottish philosopher David Hume (1711-1776) is a transitional figure who set the stage for Kant, the central figure. Like Locke, Hume held that all human knowledge is based on our sensory experience of the world. Unlike Locke, Hume did not think this knowledge could be extended by reason to claims about God or other religious matters. Hume was deeply skeptical about religious claims, whether based on revelation or reason, and in his writing he ridiculed both orthodoxy and deism with equal savagery. His most pointed attack appears in his *Dialogues Concerning Natural Religion*, published after his death.

The *Dialogues* create an imaginary conversation among three characters, two of whom represent the prevailing religious views of Hume's day, orthodoxy and deism. The third character is the skeptic (Hume). Since Hume is a figure of the Enlightenment, you might think he would be sympathetic to deism. But in the *Dialogues*, the skeptic undertakes a sustained attack on both of the others. In fact, the attack on deism is more scathing than the attack on orthodoxy, and at several points the orthodox believer is aligned with the skeptic against the rationalist.

Hume's point is that the claims of rational religion, such as its argument for the existence of God, exceed the bounds of reason. The deists, in other words, were getting ahead of themselves.

Hume noted that in worldly matters we appeal to common sense and experience, which support the conclusions we reach. But in theological matters, we move "quite beyond the reach of our faculties." The only sensible religious stance, according to Hume, is one of "refined skepticism."

The work of Immanuel Kant (1724-1804) represents the culmination of Enlightenment thought and the starting point for several lines of nineteenth-century philosophy and theology. Kant's philosophy is too complex to summarize in a few paragraphs, even when dealing with only a few of its basic features, but some familiarity with Kant is essential to our understanding of the development of liberal theology.

To begin, Kant took Hume's criticisms seriously. Kant was a rationalist in the Enlightenment sense. That is, he affirmed the centrality of reason and was concerned with the ways human beings come to have knowledge, both of ordinary physical objects of experience and of abstract matters, what Kant called transcendental concepts, such as religious beliefs and moral obligations. He realized that reason was involved in religious and moral knowledge but knew that it was a different kind of reason than that claimed by the deists. In a sense, Kant set out to save reason from itself and in the process save religion with it. As he put it in a famous passage: "I have therefore found it necessary to deny *knowledge*, in order to make room for *faith*."

Kant's approach to this dilemma involved two basic steps. The first involved what he called a "critique of pure reason," what we would call theoretical or scientific reason, which gives us knowledge of the objects of our own experience. Kant's critique had to do with reining in the deists' "pretensions to transcendent insight" in the name of reason, and is usually described in terms of his effort to establish the limits of knowledge. One of these limits is that we are not entitled to make the kinds of religious claims made by the deists on the basis of scientific reason.

Yet Kant was a deeply religious person and wanted to be able to affirm God and other "transcendental" concepts with integrity.

For Kant, this still required the use of reason. He articulated his own dilemma in these words:

> Human reason has this peculiar fate that in one species of its knowledge it is burdened by questions which, as prescribed by the very nature of reason itself, it is not able to ignore, but which, as transcending all its powers, it is also not able to answer.

He solved this dilemma by identifying a second type of reason, which he called "practical" or moral reason.

Moral reason is what gives us knowledge of our obligations toward others. Kant accepted morality as a basic part of human living. The task he set for himself was to uncover the basic conditions, or postulates, that make morality possible. His probing into these issues led him to affirm two basic postulates: human freedom and the existence of God. For Kant, the whole idea of moral obligation made no sense unless human beings had freedom and God existed.

The need for freedom is clear enough. As David West summarizes, "The fundamental postulate of morality is freedom, since if we are not free, we cannot be held responsible for our actions, and moral judgments cannot be applied to them." Kant's claim that freedom is a postulate means that even though we can't prove the existence of freedom through scientific reason, we know that it exists. We are therefore entitled to believe in it, to accept it as a piece of our knowledge.

But why God? This is less obvious, but the application of moral reason is the same as for freedom. As Kant saw it, the moral law commands us to seek the highest good; therefore, this highest good must exist. But humans must be internally motivated to act according to the moral law; that is, to seek the highest good. In order to do this, we need to be assured that the moral law matters, that the world is in fact morally ordered. For Kant, the existence of God as a moral supreme being provided the grounding for this belief. As with freedom, we can't prove this through scientific reasoning, but we can postulate it. We are therefore entitled to believe in God because God's existence is a condition of human morality.

When Kant identified religion with a separate type of reason, he affirmed the separation of religion from science. Of course throughout modernity, science was increasingly distancing itself from religion as it reshaped our understanding of the world in ways that were incompatible with older religious views. But Kant's move provided a formal structure and sophisticated justification for the separation. It legitimated religion by giving it a rational grounding in a sense parallel to if not the same as that of science. This set the philosophical stage for the modern dialogue about the relationship between science and religion, a dialogue in which liberal theology continues to be deeply involved.

By locating religion in the sphere of moral reason, Kant was in effect making a moral argument for the existence of God. This brought ethics to the forefront of religion, and ethics has been a central feature of liberal theology from its beginning. Indeed, along with Schleiermacher, historian of liberal theology Gary Dorrien includes Kant among "the founding giants of liberal theology."

Schleiermacher's theology marks the third part of the story of rational religion. While Kant located religion in morality, Schleiermacher identified a third source of religious knowledge, an internal nonrational experiential capacity he called *feeling*. For Schleiermacher, we don't think our way to God through either scientific or moral reason. Instead, we intuitively sense the action of the universe upon us and feel compelled to respond. This is precognitive and nonrational experience. And coming hot on the heels of Kant's philosophy—perhaps the most profound analysis of human reason in Western thought—the impact of Schleiermacher's proposal was huge.

While Schleiermacher provided a new grounding for theology, he is also linked to the past in two important ways. Although his move away from reason marks a significant change in modern religious thought, it wasn't much of a change when we look at it from the perspective of the Moravian pietism in which he was raised. Like other pietistic movements, this tradition emphasized the personal and inward dimensions of religious faith, including a sense of personal relationship with God or Christ, rejecting the orthodox preoccupation with doctrinal correctness. The pietists placed greater value on feeling, sometimes referred to as the "religion of the heart." Schleiermacher eventually moved away from the pietistic tradition, but he always retained a love for its warmth and inward depth. This influence can be clearly seen in his own use of feeling as the locus of human religiousness in his mature theology.

Schleiermacher also adopted many of the Enlightenment's analytical tools, including Kant's separation of theoretical and moral reason. He continued the central Enlightenment claim that the proper source of authority in religious matters is the individual self and not any external authority. In this sense, he remains very much a modern figure.

Common Sense

A different but equally important grounding for American liberal theology is a school of thought usually referred to as "Scottish common sense." Like Kant, the commonsense philosophers were reacting in part to Hume's skepticism. They wanted to affirm a philosophical basis for religious belief and human morality in the face of Hume's scathing challenge. But they approached this task from a perspective very different from Kant's.

The central figure in this movement is Thomas Reid (1710-1796), who thought that all modern philosophy since Descartes tended toward skepticism. By beginning with radical doubt, Descartes and his followers were led to deny, or at least to doubt, the reality of the external world. Moreover, Descartes, Locke, and others held that we human beings don't perceive the world directly. Instead, our perceptions are filtered through the mind's innate capacities that arrange and order them into ideas and knowledge. Reid and his cohorts thought this was absurd because it denied the "common sense" of our everyday experience. They insisted that we do perceive the world directly through our senses and that we can trust this perception. We need not doubt that the world exists. They distrusted abstract and speculative forms of philosophical reasoning, preferring to derive knowledge from direct observation or self-evident arguments. And for them, the external world existed completely independently of our conscious awareness of it.

The commonsense philosophers also affirmed certain innate capacities of the human mind. In fact, they believed that internal or spiritual perception is as important as external sense perception. While both kinds of perception are sources of knowledge, it is the internal sense that gives us moral and religious knowledge. Francis Hutcheson (1694-1746), for example, held that human beings possess an innate moral sense, which enables us to perceive the "moral right," in the same way that our other senses allow us to perceive the external world. Welsh philosopher Richard Price (1723-1791) connected this innate moral sense to human reason and moral agency. This meant that human beings have both the capacity and freedom to develop it. Just as our intellectual and physical powers can always be improved, we humans also have the potential for moral growth. In other words, while a "rudimentary moral reason is innate...moral refinement requires education and training."

These ideas were to have enormous influence on early American liberal religious thinkers. William Ellery Channing, in particular, found a deep resonance in Scottish moral philosophy. With the commonsense philosophers, he and other nineteenth-century religious liberals affirmed an innate human moral capacity. And the notion of moral and spiritual character development became a central theme of American liberal religious thought throughout the nineteenth century.

The Limits of Modernity

Modernity was not simply an unbroken line of ever-greater individual freedom and social progress. Tensions such as the artificial separation of mind from matter and the tendency of reason to morph into rationalization meant that modernity was a mixed bag from the beginning. Two contradictions nicely summarize modernity's legacy. The rise of modernity was not universally celebrated, even when it was at its peak during the Enlightenment. On the one hand, its influence in Western culture was enormous and long-lasting. Its central ideas shaped or reshaped nearly all of our basic institutions and even our thought patterns. At the same time, in many ways these were just the ideas of a particular group of white male intellectual elites in northern and western Europe. The vast majority of ordinary people in these regions, not to mention the rest of the world, continued to hold traditional religious views. And any real personal autonomy, so highly regarded by the modernists, was in truth available only to those with means.

Modernity gave us science, technology, modern medicine, universal education, democracy, human rights, the middle class, religious freedom, and much else that we take as good. It also led to or exacerbated militarism, nationalism, rampant capitalism, bureaucratization, conquest and colonialism, and at the extremes of rationalism gone mad, totalitarianism.

One of the most disturbing contradictions of modernity is its legacy of racism. During the period celebrated as an enlightened age of reason, a colossal and violent industry built on the dehumanization and enslavement of hundreds of thousands of African people was taking place. As Cornel West notes, "The great paradox of Western modernity is that democracy flourished for Europeans, especially men of property, alongside the flowering of the transatlantic slave trade and New World slavery." West calls this "the *night* side of the Age of Enlightenment, the reality left unlit by the torch of natural reason." How can we account for this jarring inconsistency?

West argues that the ideology of white supremacy was not an aberration, the misguided notion of an unenlightened few. Instead, it was built into the very structures of modernity itself. Modernity's forms of rationality, which favored classification and order, were applied to human beings. This led to a set of racial classifications that were accepted as correct because of their apparently rational ordering. By the same token, Europeans had adopted classical Greek ideals of physical beauty, which corresponded more to European than African physical types. Non-Europeans and others who seemed different were perceived to be inferior. The lens through which modernity saw the world had no room for the notion of black equality in beauty or intellectual capacity.

These negative consequences of modernity left their mark on liberal theology. This is worth remembering when we consider some of the challenges presented to modernity, and to liberal theology, by the postmodern perspective.

The Postmodern Challenge

LIBERAL THEOLOGY IS A PRODUCT of modern culture, but modernity is not the end of the story for either theology or culture. Many observers claim that Western culture is nearing the end of modernity, and some believe we have already entered a postmodern cultural condition. Yet whether our condition is one of "late" or "post" modernity, nearly everyone agrees that we live in a world very different from that which witnessed the rise of modernity and the emergence of liberal theology more than two centuries ago.

This large-scale cultural shift raises several important questions for liberal theology. If liberalism is unavoidably linked to modernity, can it remain a viable theological option in the face of modernity's demise or radical realignment? Can liberal theology adjust to the challenges of postmodernity and still remain liberal?

The term *postmodern* is a bit slippery. It is used in different ways and in many contexts. It appears in fields such as art, literature, political theory, philosophy, and religion, and it is understood somewhat differently in each area. Yet it does carry some sense of shared meaning, otherwise we would not be able to talk about it intelligently. At the very least, we can begin with the observation that "the concept of postmodernity...alerts us to some tremendously important social as well as cultural shifts taking place at the end of the twentieth century." We might think of it as a symbol for a range of critiques and challenges to modernity in general and liberalism in particular.

Both modernity and postmodernity are simply ways of looking at the world. They provide large-scale interpretive frameworks within which we orient ourselves and come to understand our life experiences. The same is true for any large-scale worldview, whether it is Christianity or Buddhism, capitalism or Marxism. It has been wisely said, "Be careful how you interpret the world; it *is* like that." The point is that the world looks different through postmodern glasses than through modern glasses. In addition to asking whether the postmodern view offers a more accurate picture of reality, we might ask whether it offers a more helpful way of perceiving ourselves and our situation than the modern view.

We began the analysis of liberal theology by identifying the liberal mind-set that emerged out of modernity. By the same token, there is a certain postmodern sensibility that can help our understanding of the more formal characteristics of postmodernity. Trying to make sense of the postmodern sensibility is not easy. To the extent that postmodernity is now part of our social and cultural reality, its sensibility is something we all carry around with us. While it may not be shared by everyone, it has become part of our presupposed worldview. Theologian Paul Lakeland offers this description:

> The postmodern sensibility, let me suggest, is nonsequential, noneschatological, nonutopian, nonsystematic, nonfoundational, and, ultimately, nonpolitical. The postmodern human being wants a lot but expects a little. The emotional range is narrow, between mild depression at one end and a whimsical insouciance at the other. Postmodern heroes and heroines are safe, so far beyond that we could not possibly emulate them, avatars of power or success or money or sex—all without consequences. Who really expects to be like Arnold Schwarzenegger—probably the best-known and highest-paid actor in the world—or Madonna? Postmodernity may be

tragic, but its denizens are unable to recognize tragedy. The shows we watch, the movies we see, the music we hear, all are devoted to a counterfactual presentation of life as comic, sentimental, and comfortable. Reality doesn't sell. So here we stand at the end of the twentieth century, a century that has seen two world wars, countless holocausts, the end of the myth of progress, and the near-death of hope, playing our computer games and whiling away the time with the toys that material success brings.

From the perspective of a religious liberal seeking to be involved in the world, this assessment appears quite negative. It seems to celebrate a kind of carefree and even value-free attitude toward the world. Yet there are positive sides of these phenomena. Difference and otherness are held up as positive values, in line with the tolerance and support for diversity liberalism has long affirmed. And while grand idealistic visions have disappeared, there is room for focusing "a more limited but achievable attention to local initiatives." In other words,

> the postmodern can be both trivial and substantial at the same time...the difference, again, seems to be that postmodernity's nose, unlike that of modernity, is not put out of joint by the realization that what can be achieved is really quite limited.

Sociologist David Lyon also sees a positive side to the postmodern sensibility. The popular perception is that postmodern life is laced with skepticism, meaninglessness, and malaise. This view is apparent in Lakeland's characterization. Yet Lyon notes that not all postmodern attitudes share this negative outlook. "Affirmative postmodernists, while they may share some of the skeptics' critique of modernity, do not 'shy away from affirming an ethic, making normative choices, and striving to build issue-specific political coalitions.'" This affirmative posture is in line with the basic culturally involved ethic of liberal theology.

Lakeland subdivides the postmodern sensibility into three postmodern personality types, surely an oversimplification. Yet Lakeland's scheme is helpful because it corresponds in several ways to the characteristic theological responses to postmodernity we see today. This is not to suggest that theology can be correlated with personality type, yet the similarities are sometimes striking.

Lakeland's first type is what he calls the *obvious*, those who are simultaneously "the product and consumer of popular postmodern culture." This is the culture of talk shows, tabloid newspapers, gossip columns, celebrity fan magazines, professional wrestling, so-called reality TV, and the like. It includes celebrities whose primary product is their own celebrity, as well as the public who follow and even admire them. As Lakeland describes this group, "They all seem to survive, nay thrive, on a cultural diet whose nutritional equivalent is sugar and preservatives." Religious liberals may see these sorts of people in negative terms, but from a postmodern perspective, it is worth remembering that they are basically *a*moral, not *im*moral. They live without a real identity or meaning structure of their own and even without any apparent need for deeper meaning. People in this group are unlikely to become involved in politics or movements for social change.

Lakeland's second personality type is what can be called the *reactionaries*. For this group, "modernity is the enemy, defined as a mix of liberalism, moral relativism, and 'secular humanism.' These individuals are at one and the same time postmodern and premodern." They make use of the tools and products of the contemporary culture, including its sophisticated communication and information technologies, yet they "hark back to a premodern world for their basic values." These are people who never quite embraced the liberal-modern culture in the first place and are now engaged in a kind of rearguard action to recover an older set of cultural values. For them, postmodernity simply represents a further degeneration of a process that started with the Enlightenment. In religious and political terms, several perspectives may be included within this group, including fundamentalists, neoconservatives, and so-called postliberals.

The term *engaged postmodernists* or *critical participants* can describe Lakeland's third type. Members of this group know they live within a postmodern situation, accept it, and take it seriously by challenging those aspects of the new cultural reality that present difficulties. These are religious workers, human-rights workers, and peace activists—people who know they can't solve all the problems of the world but still work on those they can. They recognize that there are no guarantees that we will ever reach the right outcome or that we can know from our limited perspectives what that outcome is. They nevertheless do the best they can to relieve suffering and create a more humane and just world. This view presupposes a set of modern humanitarian values, many of which are also part of the Jewish and Christian biblical traditions. To a certain extent, these critical participants seek to carry these core modern values into the new postmodern situation. In contrast to the reactionaries, they look forward to a better future rather than backward to a better past. And unlike those in the first group, they are engaged, not disengaged. As Lakeland says, "They are critically present in and to their postmodern world."

There is a fourth group that Lakeland and most other observers of the postmodern condition don't mention. It consists of those who have been excluded from both the modern and postmodern worlds. These are the poor, the oppressed, the victims of modernity's dark underbelly of colonialism, racism, and runaway capitalism. They have not fared well in postmodernity either. They remind us that the "whimsical insouciance" and casual playfulness of the postmodern sensibility presuppose a certain degree of affluence. For this reason, it may be misleading to think of this group as representing a postmodern personality type. But they are a part of the postmodern world, and they have a stake in the social structures it creates. As liberation theologian David Batstone and his colleagues put it,

> Bluntly and tersely, the postmodern as an epochal condition underscores in its celebration of camp, kitsch, and retro the

other side of a social reality in which we wallow in private affluence while squatting in public squalor.

This reality is worth keeping in mind as we consider the various
postmodern theological options.

Philosophical Themes

It is helpful to distinguish between the philosophical discourse of
postmodernity and the social and material conditions of postmodern life. These naturally overlap, but for the purpose of understanding their relationship to liberal theology, we will look
at them separately and focus on five distinct but related philosophical themes: disorientation, the collapse of metanarratives,
the loss of certainty, the "linguistic turn," and the breakdown of
boundaries.

DISORIENTATION. Most discussions of postmodernity emphasize the problem of disorientation. This is a kind of running
theme, and it might be helpful to think of the other characteristics
of postmodernity that follow as expressing this idea in various
ways. The basic idea is that the postmodern world is fragmented.
As David Lyon explains, "Whereas the modern world tended . . . to
be held together by the routines and rules of the industrial work
world and the bureaucracy of the nation state, a sense of disintegration has set in as both time and space are in flux."

In postmodernity there are no signposts or structures to rely
on, so it is harder to find meaning and purpose; everything is relative. This sense of fragmentation also leads to a celebration of
pluralism and diversity. Things can't be unified into a meaningful
whole, but no one expects them to be. We don't all think and act
and look alike, and we are all enriched as a result.

This postmodern fragmentation undercuts some of modernity's central philosophical guideposts. At minimum, it challenges
the Enlightenment principle of universality. More than this, it
challenges the very possibility of religious meaning. Religion is

fundamentally about meaning-making and finding orientation in life. The postmodern perspective throws this into doubt. In a fragmented world, can our religious traditions continue to fulfill this role? This is an important question for all religious people, especially for liberals because of the traditional liberal stance of cultural mediation. Here, the culture itself seems to have given up the possibility of meaning.

THE COLLAPSE OF METANARRATIVES. The term *metanarrative* refers to the large-scale stories and interpretive frameworks that help us orient our lives. In both modern and premodern times, people could believe, for example, that history had a clear direction and purpose. In religious terms, this belief may have included things like ultimate salvation according to a divine plan. During and following the Enlightenment, the principle of divine providence morphed into progress, often expressed as confidence in the ability of science and technology to move us forward.

Postmodernity changes all this. In the postmodern situation, our meaning-making frameworks and traditional mythologies have become less credible. More than this, the postmodern perspective distrusts any sort of unifying story of our lives or our history. It is suspicious of all grand explanatory theories, whether the idea of God's plan, or the Marxist view of history moving toward a certain kind of social structure, or an evolutionary view of life as continually improving on itself. Postmodernity replaces grand unifying narratives with small-scale independent discourses. And since there is no common reference point, these discourses can turn neither to each other nor to a common framework for support. David Lyon writes, "Each form of discourse is forced to generate what home-made authority it can."

British social scientist Anthony Giddens refers to this phenomenon as the "disappearance of historical teleology." *Teleology* has to do with ultimate outcomes or purposes and often refers to the belief that history has a clear direction toward a particular end. Teleologies involving God's design for the universe are one example. The Marxist theory about the progression of economic structures and the ultimate collapse of capitalism is another. In the postmodern way of thinking, these sorts of teleologies have largely been abandoned. We still use knowledge of the past as a means of orienting ourselves toward the future, but the future is now regarded as open-ended, to be determined by courses of action undertaken in the present. Progress and other providential views of history are no longer viable. As Lyon puts it, "Modernity is going nowhere." Perhaps it is better to say that it is going nowhere in particular. In the postmodern world, we are no longer sure that we are moving forward or even what *forward* means.

THE LOSS OF CERTAINTY. *Epistemology* is the branch of philosophy that deals with the nature of knowledge. It asks questions like "How do we know what we know?" and "What counts as knowing something?" In the modern period, the emphasis was on finding bedrock foundations for all our knowledge. People looked for ideas that could be accepted as universal truths, which could provide the foundation on which to build further knowledge. Descartes' affirmation of his existence as a thinking being is one kind of epistemological foundation. The empiricist theory that all knowledge is based on data received by the senses is another.

In the postmodern world, these foundations have disappeared. There is no such thing as certain knowledge or ultimate truth. Things we once thought gave us firm foundations, such as universal human reason or common experience, turn out to be bounded by language and culture and gender. Everything is relativized. What we used to think of as truth is now seen as interpretation. Because of our cultural limitations, all our interpretations are only partial. And it's not just that each of us has only a partial view of some larger truth. The metaphors we commonly use, such as looking at the same light through different windows or going up the same mountain on different paths, are all challenged in postmodernity. In the postmodern way of thinking, there is no larger truth. We are all wandering around on different paths (or lost in the brush) on different mountains. We each have our own truths and our own knowledge, according to our circumstances.

This condition leaves us with more decisions to make but fewer bases for making them. "As less and less can be taken as given, so more and more responsibility is placed on the individual to account for, and act in, the world." This is a social problem as much as an individual one. As Lyon recognizes, one of the central postmodern dilemmas is how we can find "authentic post-foundational starting points for social criticism." Lyon continues,

> The postmodern context, with its emphasis on individual choice and consumer preferences, when mixed with epistemological doubt and pluralism, creates a heady cocktail that seems quickly to befuddle and paralyze. At best, only local rationales, or subgroup standpoints seem available as means of discernment and choice. It is hard to see how any (post)modern society can in any sense become a desirable habitat without coming to terms with this.

In religious terms, we are left potentially without a deep grounding or even a shared reference point for our prophetic voice. This is a critical issue for liberal theology today.

THE IMPORTANCE OF LANGUAGE. Philosophers speak of the "linguistic turn" as one of the central developments of twentieth-century thought, on a par with the "turn to the subject" during modernity. The main idea is that our beliefs and experiences are always mediated through our culture and language. This is a major shift away from one of the central principles of modernity. It means that our most basic ideas are shaped not primarily by reason and experience, but by language. As Lakeland puts it, "What can be said lays down the boundaries of what can be thought."

Because language is a social product, our ideas are now understood as largely determined by culture and even by our specific location within a particular culture. In the modern world, I could think of my experiences and ideas as universally shared among all human beings. But in the postmodern world, they are nothing more than the ideas and experiences of a straight, white, middle-aged, highly educated urban male living in early twenty-first century North America. This is, of course, one of the important lessons of feminist thought.

THE BREAKDOWN OF BOUNDARIES. Postmodern thinking tends to dissolve boundaries between categories we used to think of as clear. An interesting effect of this development is that we are less sure of the difference between what is serious and what is frivolous. The postmodern way of looking at the world tends to be more playful and to take things less seriously. This is evident in such areas as manners. There is less sense of decorum or appropriateness about dress and language than many of us remember a generation or two ago. Lyon captures this trend when he notes that "in everyday life, the postmodern may be seen in the blurring of boundaries between 'high' and 'low' culture [and] the collapse of hierarchies of knowledge, taste, and opinion." The traditional categories and distinctions are simply irrelevant. In manners, music, dress, and other areas, collage is the style of the times.

This trend is evident in religion too:

> Beliefs and practices that once were sealed within an institutional form now flow freely over formerly policed boundaries. Syncretism … is now generalized and popularized, in practice as in belief. New possibilities emerge, creating liturgical smorgasbords, doctrinal potlucks. As the sacred canopy recedes and the floating signs multiply, the problem becomes less 'how do I conform?' and more 'how do I choose?'

Even reality itself is in question. Artificial intelligence, genetic engineering, and practices such as cosmetic surgery blur the lines between reality and virtual reality. In shopping malls, the distinction between inside and outside, day and night, natural and artificial have (virtually) disappeared. The mall also reverses the social differentiation that emerged in modernity by erasing the once clear division between economic activity and leisure time activity. More importantly, our moral and ethical categories are blurred. The difference between good and bad or between right and wrong is no longer as clear as it once was. One of the effects of the postmodern tendency is the weakening of universal standards of morality. The debate among feminist thinkers and others over the issue of female circumcision or genital mutilation is a telling case in point. Many argue that this practice is grossly dehumanizing and oppressive to women and must therefore be resisted. Others argue, or at least worry, that to take this stance is to impose our cultural values on others, which we shouldn't presume to do. This kind of issue shows why this debate matters. In the larger context, the postmodern worldview involves not simply a lowering of standards, as many people think; it reflects a deeper distrust of our ability to have standards at all.

Social Characteristics

The social characteristics of postmodernity represent conditions that theology must respond to and address. While different commentators emphasize different postmodern social conditions, all agree that two are critical: a new form of consumerism and new communication and information technologies. A third condition, one not typically discussed in the academic literature, is new forms and attitudes around violence.

None of these conditions is completely new. Consumption as the driving force behind modern market capitalism and continued progress through technology have been prominent social themes throughout modernity. Violence has also been a part of modern Western culture since the European conquest of the Americas. It has been suggested that the voyages of Christopher Columbus, rather than the philosophical musings of Descartes, mark the real beginning of the modern period. In postmodernity, each of these conditions has become wildly exaggerated. And all three are "bound up with the restructuring of capitalism that has been under way since at least the last quarter of the twentieth century."

CONSUMERISM. In postmodernity, consumption is central. Our economy is no longer based on the production of goods and services but rather on the production of demand. David Lyon observes,

> If postmodernity means anything, it means the consumer society. If this position is correct, much has indeed changed, and it seems to add up to an unprecedented social condition. Indeed, even consumer *society* is a misnomer, unless by it we refer to something well beyond the conventional bounds of the nation state. Consumerism is global, not in the sense that all may consume, but in the sense that all are affected by it.

We ordinarily associate consumerism with the felt need to acquire ever-increasing quantities of material goods. But in the postmodern condition, the issue is not simply acquisition; it is commodification. This reflects an important shift in worldview. In postmodern society, everything is a commodity to be shopped for. This includes not only ordinary goods (such as cars, housing, furniture, appliances, food, clothing), or services (home maintenance, recreation, travel, financial and other types of consulting, credit). Today we also treat as consumer commodities things once considered to be public goods, private relationships, or parts of our inner spiritual identities. These include education, health care, romantic partnerships, religious community, political affiliation, and even moral codes and truth claims. The reversals are startling. Public social goods have become private commodities, while our inner personal identities have become externalized as objects.

This social reality favors those who have the economic resources and political power to make the best deals. Privatization of public goods, especially education and health care, leaves many excluded. This condition means that consumer shopping skills are critical not simply for ordinary products and services but also for acquiring a good education, finding spiritual fulfillment, and even for creating meaningful personal and social relationships. The universalizing of consumerism also affects the nature of social and political participation. As consumer choice becomes the normative social process, the "market culture displaces citizenship with consumership." Theologian and biblical scholar Walter Wink comments that "consumerism has become the only universally available mode of participation in modern society." And David Batstone notes that in the postmodern society,

> The primary mode of integration into society is not through entry into the production process, but through entering the circle of consumption, of market frenzy. Whereas for industrial capitalism being a producer was of primary importance, under globalized capital, being a consumer is the determining factor.

Becoming a productive member of society no longer means finding a job, much less a career or calling. Instead, it means being able to spend money, to consume. Our social worth is measured not by what we produce or create, but by what we buy:

> This is not a workers' economy; it is a consumer's economy. How you make your living in order to consume does not matter. What matters is that you consume and participate in the bacchanalia and frenzy of boundless and useless consumption.

Those who cannot consume are simply left behind. Poverty has always meant that basic human needs go unmet, and people without means have always had less political power. Material want and social exclusion are not unique to postmodernity, but the postmodern condition exaggerates this reality. Goods that were once considered social entitlements, such as quality education and basic health care, are now private consumer goods, increasingly unavailable to the poor. And employment, when it is

available at all, entails both diminished real income and diminished social meaning. New lines of social division are created:

> The difference is no longer between workers and bour-
> geoisie, but between consumers and the destitute—those
> who not only have nothing to sell in the labor market, but
> most importantly, those who cannot afford to buy anything.

In this new social reality, the direction of responsibility
and accountability is reversed. As citizens and members of a
community, we are responsible to the whole. As consumers, the community becomes responsible to us. Desires become needs; needs
become entitlements. We come to think of ourselves as having a
"right" to have our consumer wants satisfied. Another consequence is that style and image are more important than utility and
function. Goods are no longer about filling real needs. They have
become symbols—of status, identity, class—responding to artificially created desires masquerading as needs. Images and product
logos are themselves consumer items. The priority of image
means that even identity is now a consumer product. Personal
identities, Lyon writes,

> are constructed through consuming. Forget the idea that
> who we are is given by God or achieved through hard work
> in a calling or career; we shape our malleable image by what
> we buy—our clothing, our kitchens, and our cars tell the
> story of who we are (becoming).

COMMUNICATION AND INFORMATION TECHNOLOGIES. Modernity
witnessed the development of important communications technologies, such as the telegraph, telephone, and radio. But the
technologies of the postmodern society, including television,
electronic funds transfers, and the personal computer, are of a
different order. As with consumerism, they are advancing at an
accelerated rate. Lyon observes that the growth of these newer
technologies "is one of the most striking and transformative

changes of the twentieth century. They do not in themselves transform anything, but they contribute to the establishment of novel contexts of social interaction."

These technologies have led to the emergence of new social structures built around networks. The concept of the "network society" has become common and represents a significant change from older forms of social organization. In both premodern and modern society, institutions and associations were relatively stable and normally linked to particular locations. In contrast, the postmodern network society is dynamic, decentralized, and often globalized. Once again, important questions are raised for meaning and identity: "The network society cannot provide stable meanings and sources of identity, which once were related to associations (including churches), political parties, nation states, or local communities."

VIOLENCE. The American continents were Europeanized through the horrific violence of conquest, genocide, and slavery, and violence has been a part of modern culture and of American society ever since. Although violence is not a uniquely postmodern issue, the postmodern condition has resulted in a significant shift in our cultural attitudes toward and expressions of violence. The older external forms have not disappeared, but something else is also happening within our postmodern society.

The forms of cultural violence that were sanctioned by modern social structures were primarily what we might call public or official violence. Most were carried out by the nation-state through war, the exercise of police power, and in other "official" ways. Other forms of public violence, while not officially carried out by the state, were socially sanctioned in some way, such as lynchings and mob violence in the segregated American South (and elsewhere) and "frontier justice" in the American West. At the same time, hidden forms of private violence, such as spousal and child abuse, were probably linked to the same patriarchal attitudes. Like many socially sanctioned public expressions of violence, these "private" forms were tacitly accepted by society until relatively recently. Finally, we may include the systemic structures of oppression that linger in our society, such as racism, sexism, and homophobia. These are built on patterns of domination, and at bottom they rely on violence in both physical and psychological forms.

These structures of violence were deeply engrained in modern society, and we bring them with us into our postmodern situation. Walter Wink uses the term *domination system* to describe the social structures we live in today. The main characteristics of a domination system include power over, control, competition, exploitation, self-centeredness, and especially violence. A domination system is the complete reversal of the biblical ideal of the kingdom of God, which Wink calls "God's domination-free order." As Wink notes,

> Violence is the ethos of our times. It is the spirituality of the modern world. It has been accorded the status of a religion, demanding from its devotees an absolute obedience to death. Its followers are not aware, however, that the devotion they pay to violence is a form of religious piety. Violence is so successful as a myth precisely because it does not seem to be mythic in the least. Violence simply appears to be the nature of things. It is what works. It is inevitable, the last and, often, the first resort in conflicts.... It, and not Christianity, is the real religion of America.

This remains true in postmodern society, but postmodernity also brings a new dimension to our culture of violence. On the large scale, organized forms of political violence are no longer the exclusive province of the state. Just as global capitalism knows no political boundaries, neither does global terrorism. Like the new communications technologies, global terrorism is apparently organized around decentralized networks and "cells" rather than centralized hierarchical structures. Closer to home, violence now permeates our culture. One common example is the images of violence that constantly bombard us in movies, television, children's cartoons, video games, and many other places. It is significant that many of these are linked to postmodern technologies. Many studies have shown how harmful these images are, especially to our children. Images of violence have become normative to the point of being casual.

Another form of postmodern cultural violence can be found in the now familiar patterns of what we might call "in-your-face" behavior. The postmodern breakdown of boundaries is evident not only in our relaxed understanding of manners and appropriate social conduct but also in the upsurge of mean-spirited public behavior. This goes beyond rudeness; at bottom it reflects an impulse toward violence. Confrontation rather than conciliation or cooperation is the order of the day. This is acted out in several common ways, from taunting opponents in sporting events to road rage. An especially troubling form of this pattern is parental abuse of coaches and officials in organized sports activities for children. They may intend to demonstrate support but are really demonstrating violence.

We see similar patterns at work in the degeneration of public discourse. This is especially evident on television, though it also appears in some forms of talk radio. Programs that are ostensibly about news or public affairs are reduced to entertainment. Their style of entertainment often makes them structurally indistinguishable from violence-based fake sports programming such as professional wrestling and "gladiator" combat-type shows. The same themes appear in so-called reality TV, which celebrates mean-spirited competition that leaves only one "winner." When similar formats are adopted in public affairs programming, participation in public discourse becomes mere spectatorship. When complex public issues are reduced to sound bites and those debating them resort to shouting matches and name-calling, we lose more than content. We also lose the possibility of real understanding.

Finally, the emergence of these postmodern forms of cultural violence is linked to consumerism. Again, this is in part an exten-

sion of an old pattern. Capitalism, as the basic economic structure
of modernity, has always been a central part of the larger domination system, to use Wink's term. Nearly a century ago German sociologist Max Weber claimed that "without exception every sphere
of social action is profoundly influenced by structures of dominancy." He pointed to economics as an area where this was especially true. In Weber's terms, "The great majority of all economic
organizations...reveal a structure of dominancy." According to
Wink's analysis, economic structures within a domination system
will be characterized by exploitation, greed, and inequality. Wink
elaborates:

> The Domination System...teaches us to value power. In any
> particular society, however, power is given specific shape by
> the peculiar conditions of the time. What characterizes our
> society is the unique value ascribed to money. People in
> every age have coveted wealth, but few societies have lionized
> the entrepreneur as ours does....Modern capitalism has
> made wealth the highest value. Our entire social system has
> become an "economy."...Profit is the highest social good.

As our economic system shifts from production-based to
consumption-based capitalism, these domination structures take
on new forms. Competition continues to be a central driving force
of the economy. But the locus of competition—and the violence
inherent in it—has expanded to include consumers as well as producers. In the postmodern consumer culture, we are encouraged
to compete with and ultimately to defeat each other, to think first
of our own needs, and to get all we can. An economic system that
relies on self-interested competition and ultimately reduces everything to a commodity necessarily produces domination. And with
domination comes violence in all its forms. Poet and essayist
Wendell Berry sums up nicely:

> Let us have the candor to acknowledge that what we call "the
> economy" or "the free market" is less and less distinguishable

from warfare. For about half of this century, we worried about world conquest by international communism. Now with less worry (so far) we are witnessing world conquest by international capitalism.... Its tendency is just as much toward total dominance and control.

What sort of theology is possible within a postmodern framework? What shape might a postmodern liberal theology take? How might it respond to the conditions identified above? These are important questions as we move into the third century of the liberal theological tradition.

A variety of postmodern theologies have appeared in recent years. Some represent efforts at reconstructing liberal theology in light of postmodern developments; others are highly critical of liberal theology. In order to understand their relationships with liberalism and with each other, we will classify these postmodern theologies into four groups: late-modern liberal theologies, deconstructionist theologies, countermodern theologies, and liberation theologies.

Late-Modern Theologies

The liberal theological tradition we have already described represents the late-modern theologies. It is discussed as a separate category here to make the point that most liberal theologians today have already adjusted to postmodern realities. In general terms, they seek to continue the basic project of modern liberalism, but from a more critical perspective. They are aware of the negative consequences of modernity, and they accept such postmodern principles as relativity, the problem with metanarratives, the role of language, and the mistrust of autonomous subjectivity. They understand that it may not be possible to arrive at universal truths, but for them, this doesn't mean there are no meaningful ideas or truths. Many still seek to articulate a basic narrative or set of meaningful reference points that can help us locate ourselves in the universe and provide a basis for morality. They accept the fact that our frameworks of meaning are human constructions, and they see this sort of construction as our principal theological task.

Representative figures of this group include such leading liberal theologians as Sallie McFague, Gordon Kaufman, and others whose work has been discussed throughout this book. As with theologians in any group, there are wide differences in their methodologies and their understandings of central theological categories such as God and the church. But they share the liberal commitment to deep engagement with the culture. In this sense, they represent a theological counterpart to the postmodern personality type referred to as "engaged participants." Lakeland argues that in the postmodern context, this mediating approach makes their faith less secure. But an insecure faith—a faith without certainty—is simply one of the recurring tensions within liberalism.

Deconstructionist Theologies

The theologians of the deconstructionist group are located primarily within the academic community rather than the church. Lakeland quips that this is the theological camp "with the fewest tents." Thinkers in this group more or less assume that modernity has run its course, and good riddance. Their program is to deconstruct modernity by showing that its ideas and assumptions are incoherent or circular and self-referential. They typically incorporate into their work most of the postmodern themes discussed earlier: Ideas we take as fundamental or self-evident are really contingent and relative; nothing is fixed; there are no sure reference points; everything we take to be "fact" is instead merely "interpretation." This approach represents a wholesale attack on all ideas of religious truth, including the idea of God. Many deconstructionists also seek to reveal and challenge the hidden dimensions of power that shape our ways of thinking, often without our being aware of them. Writers in this group tend to see claims of truth (religious or otherwise) as basically nothing more than legitimized power.

Most of the theologians who work from this perspective eventually give up the possibility of doing theology altogether, although they may continue to be interested in the role of religion in society. A prominent example is philosopher and religious scholar Mark C. Taylor. After developing a radically deconstructionist "a/theology" in an early work, his writings turned toward aesthetics and more recently to nontheological religious study. Sharon Welch has followed a somewhat similar path, moving from "a feminist theology of liberation" in her first book, to a "postmodern humanism" that celebrates "ethics without virtue, and spirituality without God" in a more recent work. She apparently no longer thinks of herself as a theologian, yet her recent work is theological in the broad sense of this term. And while she draws on many deconstructionist themes, her theological trajectory begins with liberalism and moves toward constructive liberation theology rather than toward deconstructionist "a/theology."

These deconstructionist approaches typically include sophisticated philosophical analyses, and they often enrich academic theological discussions in interesting ways. Many of them emphasize humor and play, and Taylor, among others, is fond of creating puns and other clever word games using theological and philosophical terms. In this sense, deconstructionists represent a philosophical counterpart to the whimsical postmodern personality type mentioned above. Yet this comparison is not really fair. The disengaged postmodern popular personality would not bother with the kind of rigorous textual and cultural analysis often undertaken by the deconstructionists. Many have offered important insights into contemporary society, and some liberal theologians have drawn on their work, but in the end, their tendency to give up on theology and even on the possibility of human meaning suggests that the road they are on ultimately leads nowhere. In this sense, they are not a deep resource for an engaged, constructive postmodern liberalism.

Countermodern Theologies

At the opposite end of the theological spectrum from the deconstructionists are theologians who tend to be highly critical of modernity and therefore of the liberal theology that goes along with it. They are also critical of many aspects of postmodern culture and see postmodernity's abandonment of any basis for meaning as especially troublesome. In many ways, members of this group want to go back to a kind of harmony or security they see as having prevailed before modernity arose. Modernity destroyed this harmony, and postmodernity is simply pointing out the inherent weaknesses of modernity that are now apparent. For this reason, Lakeland refers to them as "nostalgics." However, it is important to note that the theologians in this group are not fundamentalists. "They are, rather, theologians who are frequently fully conversant with the products of both modern and postmodern thought, secular and religious, consciously 'writing against' it." Two important contemporary theological trajectories within this group are known as radical orthodoxy and postliberal theology.

RADICAL ORTHODOXY. With the publication of Anglican theologian John Milbank's book *Theology and Social Theory: Beyond Secular Reason* in 1990, radical orthodoxy sprang onto the theological scene. This particular theology is so dogmatic in its claims and extreme in its response to modernity that it is difficult to engage it. Its sworn enemy is the modern secularism it sees as having captured and corrupted Christian theology. Liberal theology, because of its method of cultural mediation, is a prime example. From the radical orthodox perspective, even the conservative neoorthodoxy of Karl Barth goes too far. In opposition to liberalism, Barth refused all cultural accommodation, including the rationality of the Enlightenment, instead grounding his theology expressly in divine revelation. For Milbank, however, the very separation of revelation and reason leaves open the possibility "of allowing worldly knowledge an unquestioned validity in its own sphere." Milbank wants to deny modern reason any independent space of its own. Thus, radical orthodoxy sees itself as transcending "the modern bastard dualisms of faith and reason, grace and nature." But it overcomes these dualisms not through the mediating approach of modern liberalism but by returning to the premodern theology of figures such as Augustine and grounding all knowledge in God. From the radical orthodox perspective, "every discipline must be framed by a theological perspective; otherwise these disciplines will define a zone apart from God, grounded literally in nothing." Lakeland observes that "Milbank's manifesto is a shameless reassertion of the premodern superiority of Christendom."

In *Theology and Social Theory*, Milbank announces his intention "to overcome the pathos of modern theology, and to restore in postmodern terms, the possibility of theology as a metadiscourse." In this task, he undertakes a complex and sophisticated analysis of many of the central themes and figures of modern philosophical and social thought while maintaining a strict posture of rejection throughout. None of the modern insights into the human condition, whether offered by sociology, psychology, or cultural anthropology, is of any value to theological reflection. Thus, despite the depth of his analysis, he does not truly engage these disciplines. Instead, he merely scolds. As Lakeland says, "Milbank wants it both ways: namely, to assert the superiority of the Christian metanarrative, and not to have to justify its claims in the open court of reason." More than this, theological ethicist James Gustafson argues that "the blanket dismissal of various sciences to explain human nature and activity, and particularly religion and religious activities, is simplistic." Gustafson asks, for example, whether ministers and others involved in pastoral caregiving should ignore the insights of modern psychology or, say, medical or scientific explanations of tragic events. To ask these sorts of questions is to point out radical orthodoxy's failure.

In the end, this view is not simply a critique of liberalism; it is a full-scale retreat from the modern world. In a sense it represents a theological counterpart to the "reactionary" postmodern personality type. Like it, this view rejects modernity and seeks to recover an older set of norms. Yet radical orthodoxy goes far beyond a nostalgic vision of the past. As Gustafson reminds us, "To seek to avoid traffic from the sciences and other secular learning that impinges on religious routes by accepting assumptions of [radical orthodoxy] is to retreat into a sectarian religion." This view is so foreign to the liberal theological spirit and so rigid in its rejection that it leaves little space for constructive dialogue. More importantly, while its theological critiques of the modern sciences may make for interesting intellectual discussion in the academic world, it offers little to concerned religious seekers, those who live in the postmodern world and are struggling with questions of meaning and faith, those who seek guidance but not rigid dogma.

POSTLIBERAL THEOLOGY. Like radical orthodoxy, "the fundamental motivation for postliberal theology is to stem and reverse the tide of theological liberalism," writes Lakeland. Unlike radical orthodoxy, postliberal theology engages and incorporates the learning of other disciplines. It offers an important critique of liberal theology, but does so by drawing on the central themes of postmodern thought rather than on Augustinian and other premodern theologies. For this reason, its critique of liberalism is worth taking seriously.

The central figure in the postliberal movement is Lutheran theologian George Lindbeck, and its manifesto is his 1984 book *The Nature of Doctrine*. Lindbeck's challenge to liberalism begins with his understanding of the nature of religion. For Lindbeck, religion is a "cultural-linguistic" phenomenon. By this, he means that religion provides a large-scale framework that enables us to organize our experience through a set of interpretive reference points. This framework always exists within particular historical communities and traditions. From this perspective, to be religious does not mean to hold certain kinds of beliefs or to have particular kinds of experiences. To be religious is to internalize a specific tradition and live by reference to its particular framework of meaning.

At one level, there is nothing new here. Lindbeck is simply restating the functional approach to the study of religion that emerged a century ago and is represented today by figures such as cultural anthropologist Clifford Geertz and sociologist Peter Berger. Lindbeck's significant move is to extend this cultural view of religion to theology. The central task of theology, according to Lindbeck, is to "give a normative explication of the meaning a religion has for its adherents." This is basically a descriptive task, and theology is to be evaluated by how faithfully it adheres to its own narrative tradition. As Lindbeck notes, this approach tends to "result in conservative stances," although it need not do so.

In order to see how this perspective becomes a critique of liberal theology, we need to examine what Lindbeck calls the "experiential-expressive" view of religion. This is Lindbeck's term for the liberal-modern understanding that religion is grounded in certain preconscious or unmediated forms of human experience. Schleiermacher's notion of a "feeling of absolute dependence" is the defining modern expression of this view. Twentieth-century examples include William James's famous definition of religion as the feeling of apprehending oneself as being in relation to the divine and John Dewey's understanding of "the religious" as a particular quality of experience. In this view, religion is seen as internalized, located primarily within the individual human subject.

Lindbeck rejects this "experiential-expressive" view of religion because it fails to recognize its own cultural and historical location. This inward-looking understanding of religion is not universal, as liberals have traditionally liked to claim. Instead, it simply reflects a particular view of the human subject that has come to dominate Western thinking during the past two or three centuries. At a deeper level, Lindbeck challenges the primacy of religious experience itself. Instead, his "cultural-linguistic" view reverses the priority and holds that religious experience has meaning only in terms of the cultural and linguistic framework in which it is embedded. Here, Lindbeck is following the postmodern linguistic turn. Finally, Lindbeck challenges the traditional liberal understanding of the self as an autonomous, rational being who can fully develop only by freeing itself from the bondage of the social group. Lindbeck again reverses the liberal priority by making the community primary and seeing the self not as autonomous but only in relation to the communal context.

For Lindbeck and other postliberals, liberalism threatens a loss of religious identity by undermining Christianity's particularity. By identifying religion with personal feeling and downplaying the role of the religious community, liberal theology "empties out the specificity of the tradition and substitutes a vapid lowest common denominator. In the end, all religions become forms of enjoining the golden rule." Postliberalism, in contrast, turns to the tradition as a basis for a "constructive critique that relativizes both modernity and postmodernity."

From one perspective, Lindbeck is simply fighting old battles. Nearly all theologians today, including most liberals, would agree with Lindbeck that theology is always limited by its cultural context and its historical circumstances. In fact, the earliest clear expression of this principle came not from a conservative postmodern theologian but from one of the great liberal-modern theologians, Ernst Troeltsch, a century ago. Contemporary liberal theologian Gordon Kaufman has continued this historicist emphasis, adopting what might have been called a cultural-linguistic understanding of religion even in his earliest work, long before Lindbeck's model appeared. Thus, contemporary liberal theology has long since moved beyond its older universalizing and individualistic commitments.

A more interesting part of Lindbeck's program is its emphasis on tradition. The Enlightenment's rejection of all external authority, especially the church, has led to a tendency among liberals today to downplay the value of tradition as a resource for theology. Kaufman, for example, has argued that "theologians dare not simply take over traditional ideas" uncritically. Other liberals, such as theologian Henry Nelson Wieman, have emphasized the importance of religious tradition, noting that transmission of the "new order" established by ongoing divine creativity takes place through "continuing community." At the same time, Wieman warned against the uncritical acceptance of tradition. Of course freedom from the strictures of the past is often liberating, and no religious liberal would likely advocate a return to old authoritarian frameworks. It would be a mistake for liberal theology to follow Lindbeck's tendency to insulate the tradition from the larger society. But religious liberals often go too far in the opposite direction. Many liberals resist seeing themselves as part of an ongoing, living tradition out of fear of losing their sense of independence. This important piece of liberalism's identity tension is based on a false understanding of the self and perhaps an inadequate understanding of the role of tradition. One's religious tradition need not be a prison; it can also be a resource. Ironically, liberals could deepen their sense of personal fulfillment by understanding how their own tradition has helped to shape their identities.

Liberation Theologies

The umbrella term *liberation theology* includes several theological orientations. All liberation perspectives share a commitment to exposing and overcoming the causes of oppression. This commitment arises out of a practice of solidarity with victims of oppression, and it is often expressed in terms of a praxis of identification with those on the "underside" of history. This means that liberation theology's starting point is the actual, lived experience of oppression and suffering in the world.

Liberation theology has an ambiguous relationship to postmodernity. Like postmodernity, it offers a critique of modernity's grand narratives of progress, but it does so from the perspective of those who were left out of that narrative. It is the theological counterpart to the fourth postmodern personality type mentioned above, those who have been excluded from both modernity and postmodernity. It therefore operates as a critique of many aspects of postmodernity. Liberation theology is grounded in a narrative of emancipation that becomes the basis for hope. Postmodernity distrusts this form of metanarrative and thus seems to deny the possibility of ultimate hope. For this reason, Batstone suggests that postmodernity may be "toothless in the face of oppression."

Liberation theology also has an ambiguous relationship to modern liberal theology. Like liberalism, it fully engages the culture and draws on the social sciences and other cultural sources in its work. Because it speaks from the underside of history, it also operates as an important critique of both modernity and liberal theology. A viable postmodern liberal theology needs to fully engage this critique. This is so important that an entire chapter of this book will be devoted to this task.

The Problem of the Self

How do we understand ourselves as human beings? What is the basic nature of our existence? How might we describe our fundamental relationship to the universe or to God? To the planet Earth? To the society in which we live? To other human beings as individuals? As theologian Sallie McFague puts it, what is "our place in the scheme of things?"

These are big questions. In the past, they were often approached as the question of the "nature of man." Today, theologians treat these matters under the concept of "theological anthropology." Many theologians work out elaborate theories or descriptions of what it means to be human today. Some rely on biblical models, others turn to ancient or modern philosophy, and many draw on contemporary science as sources or reference points for their theological efforts.

These issues are not just important for those of us who think of ourselves as theologians. We all carry views about who we are as human beings. We may or may not think consciously or intentionally about these views often, but they are with us just the same. These deep-seated ideas shape our basic sense of what it means to be alive. Religious liberals have historically emphasized individual autonomy and personal freedom in their understanding of the human condition. This view, often called the subjectivist paradigm, is grounded in the modern understanding of the human subject. It is precisely this paradigm that has become problematic in several important ways.

Individualism versus Community

Modern Western philosophy involved a "turn to the subject" that defined the human self largely in terms of individual reason and self-awareness. As a child of modernity, liberal theology inherited this view. Several things are worth paying attention to here. First, the self is conceived as abstract and disembodied consciousness. This attitude has led to the artificial separation of mind and matter, the self separated from both its own body and the world. Second, the individual is self-authenticating: Because I am aware of myself as a rational being (I think, therefore I am), my existence is validated and justified by my own internal processes. No external authority or confirmation is needed. Third, this means that my sense of purpose or meaning must come from within myself and not from my community. The self, in effect, defines itself. In the modern view, the individual becomes a mature self, an autonomous ego, by throwing off the constraints of the social group and breaking free. This view still expresses the dominant self-understanding among religious liberals.

Today the problem of individualism is usually framed in terms of a dichotomy between the individual and the community. Recent studies have linked the rampant individualism in our culture with a disturbing loss of community. Perhaps the most important and influential study is found in *Habits of the Heart*, first published two decades ago. Sociologist Robert Bellah and his colleagues expressed concern that American individualism "may have grown cancerous," eroding the social fabric that keeps its destructive tendencies in check, and "that it may be threatening the survival of freedom itself." More recently, Robert Putnam, in his superb study *Bowling Alone*, documented the drastic reduction of "social capital," the social networks and organizations that historically provided the underpinning of a trusting and fulfilling community life in every sector of American society.

Religious communities are not immune from these trends. Indeed, in many ways, they mirror them. This is an especially important issue for religious liberals because of their historical emphasis on the individual. A 1998 survey of more than 10,000 Unitarian Universalists, perhaps the most liberal of American denominations, shows how deeply individualism runs. For example, one question asked, "What role has your congregation played most importantly in your life?" By far the largest single response was, "It supports my views and upholds my values," the most individualistic of the possible choices.

This pattern was repeated in other responses. When asked what factors most influenced one's decision to join a Unitarian Universalist congregation, more than sixty percent said "searching for a belief system and faith community that made sense to me." When asked what values the congregation should instill in children, 70 percent selected "a sense of their inherent worth, self-respect" as their first choice. And to the question "What do you expect to happen for you when you attend a Unitarian Universalist worship service?" the two largest responses, nearly equal in number, were "to remember with gratitude and celebrate what is most important in my life" and "intellectual stimulation." These sorts of responses were consistent across all demographic and theological lines, and they reflect the strong individualism, almost a self-centeredness, that seems to dominate many liberal congregations today.

Alternative views were also expressed, of course. In the question about the role of the congregation in one's life, the second largest choice, at 25 percent, was "It is a beloved community of forgiveness, love, and spiritual growth." And two-thirds named "shared values and principles" as the "glue" that binds individuals and congregations. Community is also important in times of crisis. When asked "How does being a Unitarian Universalist sustain you in times of crisis, tragedy, or pain?" nearly half the respondents chose "It provides a community of love, support, and renewal." These and other similar responses reflect a latent longing for a deeper sense of community. But Bellah, in his analysis of this survey, points out that "though values and principles are shared all right, what is shared is still fundamentally individualistic." Indeed, over 40 percent chose "acceptance, respect and support for each other as individuals" as the relevant congregational "glue."

Because Unitarian Universalism lies on the far-liberal end of the American religious spectrum, this survey may not fairly represent the larger situation within liberal religion in the United States. It would be interesting to see a similar survey of Congregationalists, Methodists, or Presbyterians. The results would likely be similar. A 1978 Gallup poll, reported in *Habits of the Heart*, "found that 80 percent of Americans agreed that 'an individual should arrive at his or her own religious beliefs independent of any churches or synagogues.'" Based on this and other evidence, Bellah and his colleagues concluded that "most Americans see religion as something individual, prior to any organizational involvement."

The problem goes deeper than liberal religion. Individualism lies at the core not only of liberal religion, but of American culture itself. As Bellah notes, one of the central characteristics of American culture "is the sacredness of the individual conscience, the individual person." This cultural reality leads to the unavoidable conclusion that "what religious liberalism and American culture generally lack is a social understanding of human beings. We start from an ontological individualism, the idea that individuals are real, society is secondary." This perspective unavoidably colors our attitudes toward religious community.

Many of us share the widespread concern about the dwindling sense of community in American life, and some are especially concerned with the role of religious community. We say we want stronger communities, yet we seem afraid to let go of the individualist orientation that stands in the way. A shared belief in autonomous individualism is a poor foundation on which to build a deeper sense of community, religious or otherwise. Here we will focus not on the problem of community as such, but rather on the individual side of the equation.

The deep-seated individualism in our culture—and in religious liberalism—reflects a misguided and dangerously outmoded understanding of the human self. We cannot adequately satisfy our longing for community until we learn to embrace a different view of the self. The importance of balancing the needs of the individual and the community will always be there. But the balance we strike, indeed our attitudes toward community itself, is affected by our self-understanding. We don't need simply to shift the balance between the individual and the community; we need to come to a different notion of what it means to be an individual. We will not make much progress toward reclaiming the community we seek unless we grasp this.

The liberal-modern individualistic understanding of the self, though still widely held in liberal religious circles, is no longer tenable. It is rooted in an outdated philosophical paradigm and inconsistent with contemporary developments in the natural and social sciences. This idea is itself the product of a particular culture. In many ways, it is a historical anomaly. In other words, our liberal-modern understanding of ourselves as autonomous individuals is an illusion. The truth is that we don't first exist as individuals who then form social groups. The group always comes first. As individuals, our identities are always formed in relation to a particular social context. We are social beings through and through.

The Social Self

The Enlightenment view that placed the rational autonomous being at center stage did not go unchallenged, even within modern philosophy. During the nineteenth century, precisely as liberalism was becoming the dominant modern theology, several alternative voices began to emerge. Together these voices came to form what has been called a philosophical counterdiscourse to the dominant Enlightenment view. This counterdiscourse called into question the self's elevated place in the modern scheme of things. It was nearly a century before liberal theologians began to adjust to this development. The self was "decentered" in several important ways. These new perspectives did not (yet) replace subjectivity with intersubjectivity; the individual was still the relevant reference point. But they did challenge the individual's claim to autonomy and disinterested or "objective" rationality. Modernity's soft underbelly, we might say, began to be exposed.

The challenge to the autonomous individual took place along several simultaneous fronts that helped set the stage for the radical challenges that were to come during the twentieth century. The first important move was made by German philosopher G. W. F. Hegel (1770-1831), who saw all individual entities, including human beings, as particular manifestations of a larger, all-encompassing Absolute. This Absolute revealed itself through an ongoing historical process. In this perspective, the individual is subordinated to the inexorable movement of this larger historical process. The self's place in the scheme of things is therefore reduced.

Karl Marx (1818-1883) also saw a historical process at work but inverted Hegel's view. For Marx, this historical process belonged not to some transcendent ideal but in the earthly material realm. The human being is embedded in the material world of human ideology and social class. This insight challenged both the autonomy and the privileged status of the individual. It also reminded us that our ideas always come from somewhere. We aren't as independent of our social contexts as we sometimes like to think.

Later in the century, German philosopher Friedrich Nietzsche (1844-1900) further subverted our pretense of reasoned rationality, which he called our Apollonian side, by forcing us to confront our long-repressed nonrational or Dionysian side. This nonrational dimension of the self includes an urge to creative expression and a will to power, neither of which are grounded in reason. In effect, Nietzsche showed us that we humans are more complex beings than Enlightenment rationalists wanted to admit. Sigmund Freud (1856-1939) expanded on this same insight by turning the subject inside out and showing how the rational conscious mind is largely dominated by the hidden messages and urgings of the subconscious mind.

As important as these developments were, they did not completely dethrone the Enlightenment idea of the self. Instead, they were warnings against an uncritical faith in objective rationality and overconfidence in the powers of the autonomous subject. A true break with the philosophy of subjectivity, one that saw the individual not only as decentered but also as derivative, came in the early decades of the twentieth century with the social psychology of American pragmatists John Dewey (1859-1952) and George Herbert Mead (1863-1931). This approach rejected the idea of the autonomous self and instead argued that the human self is an inherently social being. Philosopher and cultural critic Cornel West has referred to this development as "an intersubjectivist turn which highlighted the communal and social character of acquiring knowledge." These ideas have helped to shape the modern understanding of the self and in turn affected the way we now think about theology.

Dewey held what we could call an organic view of the self. It is rooted in natural processes, especially in the dynamic relationship between an organism and its environment. In this relationship, a mutually beneficial exchange takes place in which both the organism and its environment continually influence each other's development. While this can be seen clearly in biological exchanges, Dewey sees the same process at work at the human level. Like other animals, human beings are always found in groups. They exist within both a natural and a social environment that sets the conditions on which they depend for their existence and growth. At the same time, the dynamic mutuality of the relationship means that human activities also continually alter and, to an extent, create these environments. Dewey rejects both unfettered individual freedom and a strict determinism that denies any room for individual initiative. Instead, he finds a middle ground that affirms human independence within natural, cultural, and historical limits:

> We can recognize that all conduct is *interaction* between elements of human nature and the environment, natural and social.... Freedom is found in that kind of interaction which maintains an environment in which human desire and choice count for something. There are in truth forces in man as well as without him.

Dewey develops this organic understanding of the self by means of the twin concepts of *habit* and *impulse*. A habit is a predisposition or tendency to act in certain ways. We develop habits as we learn behaviors that satisfy our needs. For Dewey, habit is as much a social phenomenon as an individual trait. It also expresses the mutuality of organism and environment. Just as breathing is as much "an affair of the air as ... of the lungs," so human habitual activities are functions of the environment (social and natural) as well as of the human agent. This is because habits are always taught by the group. They are an essential feature of the process of socialization; they teach the human infant what it means to be human within the context of a particular group. In habit formation, the group "is always accessory before and after the fact."

For Dewey, it is a mistake to think that social customs, or collective habits, are formed by the accumulation of individual habits. Individual activities (habitual or otherwise) do affect the group, but the primary influence is the other way around:

> To a large extent customs persist because individuals form their personal habits under conditions set by prior customs. An individual usually acquires the morality as he inherits the speech of his social group. The activities of the group are al-

ready there, and some assimilation of his own acts to their pattern is a prerequisite of a share therein, and hence of having any part in what is going on. Each person is born an infant, and every infant is subject from the first breath he draws and the first cry he utters to the attentions and demands of others. These others are not just persons in general with minds in general. They are beings with habits, and beings who upon the whole esteem the habits they have, if for no other reason than that, having them, their imagination is thereby limited. The nature of habit is to be assertive, insistent, self-perpetuating.

This leads to a view of the relationship between the individual and society that is the reverse of the usual modern view. Dewey rejected as artificial the traditional philosophical problem of how individuals come to form a society. The simple reality is that "some preexistent association of human beings is prior to every particular human being who is born into the world." The important problem is not how society is formed, but rather to discover the ways in which these ingrained patterns of group interaction affect the individuals who are caught up in them, as well as the ways in which individuals continuously remake and redirect them. For Dewey, this is the central inquiry of social psychology.

Yet habit is not the only influence on human activity. Even the infant brings something to the process. Dewey rejected the idea, popular in his day, that human infants are essentially passive creatures who need social or parental prodding to become active beings. Instead, the human infant is "a bundle of energy which will express itself in movement, come what may." This energetic nature is attributable to what Dewey variously calls impulses, or instinctive activities, or native tendencies. While there is a more or less "native stock" of these instinctive tendencies among humans, this does not mean that all people react alike to similar situations. Impulses are simply highly flexible starting points. They may be expressed and channeled in many different ways. Fear, for example, may be expressed as cowardice, caution, respect, or awe. This depends on how a particular impulse is mixed with others and also on the "outlets and inhibitions supplied by the social environment."

Impulses are also the starting point for the socialization process. While impulses are in a sense prior to habits because they are part of the human endowment at birth, they are also secondary and dependent. Infants are themselves dependent beings. They owe to adults not only procreation and protection but also "the opportunity to express their native activities in ways which have meaning." Thus, "the *meaning* of native activities is not native; it is acquired. It depends upon interaction with a matured social medium." The interplay of impulse and habit is an expression of what Dewey has called the "ambivalent character" of human nature, "the conjunction...of whimsical contingency and lawful uniformity."

While Dewey's understanding of the self is unquestionably a social one, he maintains an abiding concern with human individuality and personal development. This is a social process, yet it is one in which the individual eventually distinguishes itself from the group. Using Dewey's terms, we can say that impulse has a tendency to pull against habit. It is the key to both individual development and social change. As Dewey put it, impulses are the "agencies of deviation" or "the pivots upon which the reorganization of activities turn." They are the "agencies for transfer of existing social power into personal ability; they are the means of constructive growth."

Finally, it is important to note that Dewey's concept of *self* is itself a dynamic and functional concept, not a substantive or metaphysical one. Because the self emerges out of a social context dominated by habit or custom, it is a highly complex phenomenon that is always growing. Moreover, for Dewey, there is no such thing as a "separate individual mind" or an "original separate soul." These sorts of notions artificially separate human beings from their natural and social contexts. Dewey mocked the theological concept of "the unity and ready-made completeness of the soul," claiming that selfhood is full of inconsistent and unharmonized tendencies. The self is not fixed but always "in process of making."

G. H. Mead's social psychology has played a central role in the emergence of the new philosophical paradigm of intersubjectivity. In several ways, Mead's conception of the self is similar to Dewey's. Like Dewey, Mead denied the existence of any "substantive soul" or other such faculty that exists from birth. He also saw the self as a process that develops through social experience and activity. The continuous interaction between self and society, both at the organic and the linguistic-communicative levels, permits the self to emerge. Self and society create one another. Here, too, Mead was in agreement with Dewey.

In many ways, Mead's conception of the self is more radical than Dewey's. For Mead, the self is social at every level. Mead reversed the modernist philosophy of subjectivity that sees the autonomous self as primary and the society as a derivative collection of individuals. Instead, individual selves are derivative of the social process in which they exist. The social order is both a logical and a biological precondition of the existence of individual selves, which always belong to and emerge out of that social order. Selves never exist in isolation; they "can only exist in definite relationships to other selves." At both the social and biological levels, the individual is formed through a social and communicative process.

The radical intersubjectivity of Mead's conception can be seen in his notion of "taking the attitude of the other." Mead's social psychology challenges the modern view of the experiencing individual that originated with Descartes. For Mead, the individual can experience herself only indirectly, either from the perspective of other members of the same social group or from the standpoint of the group as a whole, which Mead referred to as "generalized other." In other words, the individual's experience of herself is not first as a subject, but as an object, in the same way that she experiences others as objects.

Mead used the concepts of the "I" and the "me" to distinguish the self as subject and the self as object. These are related, but in Mead's theory, the "me" comes first. That is, the self first emerges by means of "taking the attitude of others." The "I" emerges as the individual responds to or reacts against the social situation within which he is located. The subject or "I" becomes part of one's experience only after one has acted. The result is that even the "I" self—the experiencing subject—is a social or intersubjective phenomenon.

The "I" contains what Mead called a novel element that involves a sense of freedom or creativity. This idea corresponds in some ways to Dewey's understanding of impulse. As humans develop, the "I" seeks to express itself over against the "me." The "me" belongs to the group and therefore represents the group's values. It in effect provides the structure within which individual self-expression takes place. It acts as a censor, determining the range and types of possible self-expression. But within that structure, the "I" reacts and responds so that something new is created and added to the structure. Echoing Dewey's mutuality of organism and environment, Mead stated,

> The response of the 'I' involves adaptation, but an adaptation which affects not only the self but also the social environment which helps to constitute the self; that is, it implies a view of evolution in which the individual affects its own environment as well as being affected by it....
>
> As a man adjusts himself to a certain environment he becomes a different individual; but in becoming a different individual he has affected the community in which he lives....There is always a mutual relationship of the individual and the community.

In extreme cases, the response of the "I" appears as genius. But all human beings possess and continually exercise this creative capacity in greater or lesser degrees. Thus, each self is unique, but no self can exist without the common social structure. There can be no individual "I" without the prior existence of a social "me." Both aspects of the self are necessary to full self-expression. For Mead, the self is social through and through: "It is impossible to conceive of a self arising outside of social experience."

The intersubjective paradigm finds its most important expression today in the work of German philosopher and social theorist Jürgen Habermas. Habermas agrees with Dewey and Mead that the concept of a *social* self does not preclude the emergence of a fully *individuated* self. In much of his work, Habermas attempts to clarify the social process by which this individuation takes place. He sees individualization and socialization as two sides of the same coin. Like Mead, he holds that the individual can become an individual only within a social process:

> Individualization is pictured not as the self-realization of an independently acting subject carried out in isolation and freedom but as a linguistically mediated process of socialization and the simultaneous constitution of a life-history that is conscious of itself.... Individuality forms itself in relations of intersubjective acknowledgment and of intersubjectively mediated self-understanding.

In plain English, this means that the self is formed intersubjectively, in relationship. We are not first individuals who then form social groups. Instead, not only do our groups always precede us, but we become selves in the first instance through the process of social interaction. For Habermas, as for Dewey and Mead, "personal identity essentially involves social identity and the constitution of the self is concomitant with the establishment of relationships in the context of a shared lifeworld." In other words, the self is thoroughly relational, thoroughly social.

Habermas builds on Mead's distinction of the "I" and the "me" and develops a conception of individualization that contains both universal and particular aspects. In the early stages of identity development, the particular is dominant. Here, both the "I" and the "me" are closely tied to conventional social roles. At this level, the self is largely shaped and limited by its particular social context. Individuation is limited, as the individual is concerned at this stage primarily with the capacity for participation in the social group. This is an important stage. Here the individual develops the capacity to make herself understood within the meaning structure of the group and to take a position in the context of social discourse. At this stage the individual also develops a moral identity by internalizing conventional norms and learning to use them in appropriate contexts. Habermas refers to this basic social capacity as *communicative competence.*

As the self continues to develop, it moves beyond this conventional stage and eventually enters a postconventional stage, where the universal aspect begins to emerge. The individual learns to distance herself from her social world and to make moral judgments by appealing to a larger normative framework than the norms of the group. That is, she learns to take the perspective not merely of a specific "other" in a particular context, but of a "generalized other." At this level, what is internalized is not any particular conventional social norms, but what Canadian philosopher Allison Weir calls "the ability to appeal to principles, to standards of validity." In effect, the individual's social context has been enlarged into a kind of idealized universal community. It is here that we find what Habermas calls the fully individuated self.

For Habermas, the individuated self has a strong sense of autonomy and self-determination. This sounds a lot like the old modernist conception of the individual, but it is in fact very different. In the modern view, the individual is self-determining from the start, with no need for social or group involvement. In Habermas's intersubjective view, the self is understood as a social being from the start. Identity is formed in the conventional socializing process before it can emerge into the autonomous postconventional stage. And it remains social or intersubjective, even though the relevant context has shifted to the universal community. But the individual can never begin at this universal place. We all always begin with the particular community into which we are born.

Autonomy involves an implicit demand for freedom from fixed conventions and given laws. By acting autonomously, the individual learns to orient his actions beyond existing conventions and social roles, getting some distance and perspective on them. This postconventional perspective also provides the necessary leverage for critique of one's own community. In effect the individual has now become a "larger self," an "autonomous subject who can orient his action to universal principles" rather than to the norms of the particular group.

Individuation also involves a process of self-realization. Here, individuals learn to use their autonomy to develop and express their own particularity. This also remains a social or intersubjective process, even as it reaches beyond established social conventions. Through social interaction, the individual finds the social space for self-presentation and realization of her own uniqueness. Individuation thus enables creative self-expression as well as increased self-respect and self-worth.

Most liberal theologians today have absorbed the lessons of the intersubjective paradigm. They have developed theological anthropologies that reject the older liberal-modern view of individual autonomy in favor of a fully social understanding of the self. To show how this works in practice, we will look at the work of Gordon Kaufman and Sallie McFague, two of the leading liberal theologians working today.

In his most systematic theological work, Kaufman develops what he calls a *biohistorical* understanding of the human. This view starts with an ecological and evolutionary understanding of the world. Human beings are one among countless life forms that have emerged on planet Earth over the eons, and they are radically interconnected with every other form of being. But we humans are more than biological beings, we are also historical beings who contribute to our evolutionary development by creating cultures within which we continue to shape and transform the conditions of our existence. Like the biological order, this cultural order continues to evolve. In fact, it evolves more quickly, producing greater historical and regional variations than the biological order, which has remained relatively stable for thousands of years. Kaufman thus claims that "humanity is created as much by history as by biological evolution." This is a social conception of the self, though Kaufman prefers the term *biohistorical*. This then becomes the starting point for theological reflection about what it means today to be human in the world.

Two important elements of this are human agency and the emergence of human moral consciousness. Human agency has to do with the degree to which humans may affect the larger historical and cultural forces within which they are embedded. Kaufman is clear that we humans do have agency. He reaches this conclusion not by means of any Cartesian introspection, but by examining the consequences of historical evolution. Human existence is characterized by a "prolific cultural creativity" that has produced language, customs, institutions, patterns of thought and understanding, complexes of meaning and value, and so on. None of these was created deliberately, yet none could have emerged independent of human action. Thus something more than biological impulse is involved. That "more" is what Kaufman calls intention, the fact that human beings act with purposes and goals. This human ability to act deliberately, to have and carry out intentions, is the basis of human agency.

Intentional activity also involves making deliberate choices from alternative courses of action. This means that humans are responsible for those actions, both in the sense of originating them and of being held accountable for them. "To be an agent...is not merely to be one who can do something: it is to be one who is held accountable for what he or she does, and who holds herself or himself accountable." The element of accountability leads to the emergence of moral agency, a natural product of our existence as beings who are shaped by cultural processes as well as biology.

Our existence as historical beings living in groups makes it inevitable that we develop norms to guide our social behavior.

Sallie McFague's theological anthropology is part of a larger project that involves what she calls an ecological theology. Like Kaufman, she begins with the sciences. Our theological task, she says, is to ask, "Who are we in the scheme of things as pictured by contemporary science?" In general, McFague emphasizes physics, cosmology, and ecology, whereas Kaufman emphasizes biology and the social sciences. At the largest level, she turns to what she calls the common creation story, beginning with the big bang, which links the entire universe in a common narrative.

More specifically, the metaphor—and the reality—of the body is central in McFague's theology. She often refers to her project as a theology of embodiment. She speaks of the universe or the world as God's body and focuses at every level on the physical and embodied nature of reality, including human experience. On the specifically human level, she begins with evolutionary biology: "An embodiment anthropology must start with who we are as earthly, physical creatures who have evolved over billions of years as pictured by postmodern science." From this starting point, McFague develops an understanding of the human self as fundamentally social in nature. The older liberal-modern individualistic view of the self belongs to an outmoded atomistic view of reality. We are, of course, individuals. But our well-being, our fulfillment, our very existence depends on the larger ecosystem around us:

> We are profoundly interrelated and interdependent with everything living and nonliving in the universe and especially on our planet, and our peculiar position here is that we are radically dependent on all that is, so to speak, "beneath" us (the plants on land and the microorganisms in the ocean as well as the air, water, and soil).

McFague proposes what she calls a *subject-subject* model of relationship, again rejecting the modern subject-object model. As

McFague sees it, this subject-object understanding of the self wrongly elevates and isolates the human individual. In the end, it destroys the self it celebrates because it artificially separates humans from everything they depend on and necessarily belong to. The subject-subject model, on the other hand, represents

> a basic change in sensibility from the modern post-Enlightenment confidence in the individual who, as rational man, is set over against the world, which he can both know and control. The new sensibility understands human beings to be embedded in the world—indeed, in the earth: they are social beings to the core, and whatever they know of the world comes from interaction with it.

Thus, like Kaufman, McFague rejects the older subjectivist paradigm in favor of an intersubjectivist approach that sees the human self as fully social in nature.

Agency and Context

Two tensions are inherent in liberal theology: One involves the issue of religious identity; the other involves the liberal commitment to social justice. The individualistic understanding of the self that emerged with the philosophy of subjectivity during the Enlightenment in part created these tensions. If we religious liberals could adopt the new intersubjective paradigm, if we could genuinely accept the reality that we are fully social selves, we could respond to these tensions in more constructive ways. We could maintain a stronger sense of identity as religious liberals and also provide a stronger critical grounding for prophetic and justice-oriented social witness. Nearly every contemporary theologian who has addressed this issue has endorsed a concept of the self that is fundamentally social or intersubjective in nature. The following discussion, then, can be seen as one contribution to an ongoing conversation about the understanding of the self within the liberal religious tradition.

Two basic themes have become widely shared in all recent discussions of the nature of the self. First, the self must be understood in naturalistic and organic terms. The human being is a biological organism that has evolved over many centuries through a process of continual and mutual exchange with its environment. Second, to say that the self is social is to say that the self cannot exist in isolation. It can exist only in relation to other selves. The self emerges out of a process of intersubjective exchange that always takes place within a preexisting social context. This means that individual identity is constructed intersubjectively, through participation in shared contexts of meaning. As political scientist and philosopher Seyla Benhabib puts it,

> The "I" becomes an "I" only among a "we," in a community of speech and action. Individuation does not precede association; rather it is the kinds of associations which we inhabit that define the kinds of individuals we will become.

These ideas form the starting point of what it means to say that the self is social. Using this conception as a framework, three additional themes are especially important for contemporary liberal theology. Thinking in these terms can help address both the problem of individualism and the tensions in liberal religion described above. These themes are participation, identity, and embeddedness.

PARTICIPATION. Moral agency begins with the ability of the human being to interact intentionally with others and with the natural and social environments in which one is always situated. Participation is an extension of the theme of moral agency. Kaufman suggests that the moral dimension of human agency arises with the need to choose among alternative courses of action and to be held accountable for them. But the moral dimension is also inherent in the fact that these choices are made within a social context. Agency can be expressed only in social terms, which means that interaction among social agents is the organic basis of morality.

Participation extends this idea by suggesting that moral agency involves not only communication through language, but also through action. The self emerges as one engages in activities in the world with other agent-selves in the context of concrete social situations and institutions. Participation allows us to appreciate the perspective of the other not simply by virtue of linguistic give and take but also as we encounter and engage the other in actual life situations. Ethicist Sharon Welch criticizes purely communicative approaches as inadequate without the added dimension of shared practice. She sees shared work, or "material interaction at the most basic level," as forming the basis on which emancipatory conversation can take place. In this way, shared work also leads to mutual transformation.

This participatory dimension of the social self responds to the justice tension in liberal religion. By coming to understand ourselves as social beings, liberals may come to see forms of participation such as social justice work not simply as a choice we make (or do not make) as individuals but as a fundamental factor in the formation of our own identities. In other words, we must think of social justice work not simply as something we do, but as part of who we are. If I cannot see myself in solidarity with others whose circumstances are different from my own, then something is missing from my own identity. My sense of self is incomplete. In this self-help-oriented culture, we often feel the need to attend to our own well-being before we can reach out to someone else. But the idea of participation can remind us that our own well-being is deeply connected to the well-being of others and that we can be healed only when there is healing, and justice, for others as well. Participation through shared practice also contributes to the formation of the self as a moral agent because it provides a context for applying and testing the moral norms that are inculcated through the normal socialization process.

IDENTITY. Like participation, identity is also in part an extension of moral agency. As used here, *identity* involves a sense of orientation that permits the self to take a moral stand. As philosopher Charles Taylor has noted, identity has to do with knowing who we are. This is a relational notion because who we are is always defined with reference to the social context within which our commitments and choices are made. Taylor speaks of an "essential link between identity and a kind of orientation." Thus,

> To know who you are is to be oriented in moral space, a space in which questions arise about what is good or bad, what is worth doing and what not, what has meaning and importance for you and what is trivial and secondary.

A self is more than a moral agent, more than someone who must make decisions. A self is an agent with identity, an agent who can take a moral stand within a defining community. Identity is related to participation, since self-identity "is constructed through my participation in communities, institutions, and systems of meaning," as Allison Weir writes. In other words, participation contributes to the formation of identity by mediating the formation of shared structures of meaning. And these shared structures of meaning constitute the social ground on which we are able to take moral stands.

The notion of moral identity can help address the identity tension in liberal religion. This tension is partly the result of the liberal tendency to see identification with a community as leading to loss of individuality. The liberal myth is that moral stands are arrived at through unencumbered and disembodied reason. In fact, moral stands can be understood as moral only within the context of a defining community. In the contemporary world we always belong to several overlapping communities, and morality is often ambiguous. For the religious person, one of these communities is the religious community and its tradition. If we can understand our moral agency as something that emerges only as we learn to take moral stands within our communities, we might be more willing to claim our communities as positive resources rather than as prisons that we must break free of. We can turn to the liberal religious tradition for guidance and support in our moral stances, aware that our positions are stronger when we see them as embedded in a tradition.

EMBEDDEDNESS. The reality is that human selves are always embedded in social and historical contexts. This basic fact forms a key part of the background for the themes of moral agency and identity. The notion of an embedded self emphasizes both the particularity of these contexts and the fact that these contexts exist prior to the self, both ontologically and historically.

Taylor's discussion of the language community begins with the deep relationship among language, self, and community. We cannot become selves without "being initiated into a language," and "we first learn our languages of moral and spiritual discernment by being *brought into an ongoing conversation* by those who bring us up." In other words, we are always already embedded in a language community, and this embeddedness is essential to our existence as moral selves-with-identity.

The notion of embeddedness can also help address the identity tension in liberal religion. In subjectivist and individualistic perspectives, we tend to think of our selves as both logically and morally prior to the community. We know that we are products of biological evolution and cultural conditioning, but the individualist tends to see evolution as incidental and society as a product of agreement. Moreover, we often apply this same idea to our religious self-understanding.

However, if we come to see ourselves as embedded selves, as beings who do not agree to form a society but are always already embedded in one, we might develop a different understanding of the religious tradition. When we belong to a tradition, whether we are life-long members or newcomers, we are not creating it anew. We are embedding ourselves within an ongoing movement that is already there. Just as the self is always situated within a continuously developing culture, a member of the religious tradition is always "brought into an ongoing conversation." True understanding of the social embeddedness of the self would contribute to a deeper understanding of the value of the tradition as part of the embedding context.

The principle of embeddedness can also help address the liberal justice tension. There is a telling irony here. If liberals were to adopt a fully social conception of the self, the effect would be a deeper sense of their embeddedness in their own cultural and social groups, including their own religious tradition. Since liberals see themselves as open and inclusive, this culturally defined perspective might seem to have a narrowing effect. In fact, the opposite is true. Not until we see ourselves as embedded in our own cultural circumstances will we be able to see the embeddedness of those whose circumstances are different from our own. Appreciating this embeddedness can deepen our awareness of individuals who suffer oppression and of the structures of oppression in which they are situated. Awareness of these situational differences can open our own eyes to the ways in which we are implicated in these structures, the ways in which our middle-class privilege depends on them.

This awareness of differently situated selves then becomes a vehicle for critique and a protection against the insularity of a focus limited to one's own tradition. Learning to see one's own moral identity as formed within particularized contexts contributes to the awareness that can lead to effective social justice witness in the face of structured oppression.

We liberals need to be willing to acknowledge that we are never as autonomous as we think we are. We are always products of our cultures, whatever our current place in and stance toward that culture. We need to find ways to embrace the restraining limits and the nurturing strengths of our communities, especially our religious communities. We must be willing to challenge and critique our communities as well as our larger society when critique is needed. As critics we are simultaneously inside and outside, independent and interdependent.

Coming to see ourselves as social beings does not diminish our autonomy or our sense of self. Our identities are always formed in groups, and we cannot fully develop them unless we truly recognize this reality. Understanding ourselves as social beings will only strengthen and deepen our self-understanding. At the same time, our recognition that we are always products of our cultures, even when we see ourselves as critics of that culture, can increase the power of our critical and prophetic voices.

Religious Experience
and Language

THE LIBERAL RELIGIOUS TRADITION has always had a particular understanding of the relationship between language and experience. In principle, at least, liberal theology begins with religious experience and then moves to language. The experience is normally thought of in personal or individualistic terms and is usually understood to be precognitive. Theological interpretation and expression of this experience are seen as secondary activities, subordinate in both time and importance to the experience itself. This entire approach to religious experience has been called into question by developments in postmodern thought.

In order to understand the nature of the postmodern challenge, we need to understand the liberal-modern view of religious experience. Once again, we must begin with Schleiermacher. We have already noted how Schleiermacher shifted the grounding of religion from moral reason, where Kant had located it, to experience. To oversimplify, we might say that where Kant *reasoned* his way into religion, Schleiermacher found it in a particular type of *feeling*. Several things are important to note about this shift.

Schleiermacher's proposal was more radical than it may appear to us. The publication of his famous book *On Religion: Speeches to Its Cultured Despisers* in 1799 marked the first time re-

ligion had been philosophically grounded in experience. This is
not to say that religion had not involved human experience until
Schleiermacher made his claim. As religious scholar Wayne
Proudfoot reminds us, "religion has always been an experiential
matter," not simply a set of credal propositions or ritual practices.
Human beings have experienced awe and wonder in the face of
the mystery of the universe since before recorded history, and perhaps an intuitive sense of connection with something beyond us
as well. The significance of Schleiermacher's move was to turn religious experience into an analytical category, a theological concept as well as an element of the human condition. Following
Schleiermacher, the idea that religion is fundamentally about experience became normative for modernity and in turn for liberalism. Today this view is sometimes taken so for granted that it can
be difficult to realize there was ever any other way to understand
religion.

Schleiermacher had in mind a particular type of experience.
He was not concerned (at this stage, at least) with ritual practices,
religious institutions, social ethics, or other forms of outward experience. These things might be part of the religious life, but they
did not constitute the core of religion itself. Instead, religion was a
matter of personal inward experience:

> What I assert and what I should like to establish for religion
> include the following: It springs necessarily and by itself
> from the *interior* of every better soul, it has its own province
> in the mind in which it reigns sovereign, and it is worthy of
> moving the noblest and the most excellent by means of its
> innermost power and by having its innermost essence
> known by them.

This inner reality is not a form of cognition. Schleiermacher was
careful to distinguish it from intellectual activities such as philosophical speculation and moral justification. "Religion's essence,"
as he famously put it, "is neither thinking nor acting, but intuition
and feeling." It involves a form of immediate, precognitive percep-

tion. In addition, this capacity is an inherent part of the human condition. It is in this sense universal, something available in principle to all human beings, though some will inevitably be more attuned to it than others. This means that it is not specifically linked to Christianity or to any other particular religious tradition.

This inner experience, as Schleiermacher understood it, has a specific content. The intuition and feeling from which religion emerges are not just amorphous sensations; they involve a direct perception of something. Schleiermacher described the object of this experience in various ways, commonly in phrases such as "the sensibility and taste for the infinite" and an "intuition of the universe." What we experience, then, is a quality of relationship with the universe. Religion "is just a question of finding the point from which one's relationship to the infinite can be discovered."

In his first book, Schleiermacher's understanding of religion is not linked to any concept of God. What is intuited is not God, at least not the theistic God of traditional Christian theology, but the universe or the infinite. Schleiermacher was clear that religion does not depend on the existence of any sort of divine being. On the other hand, when he turned to systematic theology in his later writings, Schleiermacher described this basic experience as a "consciousness of being absolutely dependent, or, which is the same thing, of being in relation with God." In this later writing, he spoke specifically as a Christian theologian and reinterpreted the general intuition of the universe in this specific way. For Schleiermacher, this experience of God generates a desire for more knowledge and a deeper understanding of one's faith. In other words, religious experience leads to theology. The goal of theology is to deepen our understanding of this inward experience by making it intelligible and giving it meaning. And the starting point is always found in the experience.

Finally, Schleiermacher understands this inward experience as prereflective and prelinguistic. It takes place independently of, and in an important sense prior to, any attempt to reflect on it or communicate it. As theologian Thomas M. Kelly puts it, this "original, unified, and prelinguistic experience is distinct from and inaccessible to thought and speech." This is a critical point for Schleiermacher and for the liberal theology that followed him. It means that "an experience and the subsequent reflection upon that experience are two different realities." A kind of progression is set up moving from experience, to reflection, and finally to communication through language. This produces a paradox in which we are left trying to use words to describe an experience that is itself independent of language. The result is that language is always inadequate. The underlying experience can never be fully captured. Schleiermacher laments,

> The finest spirit of religion is thereby lost for my speech, and I can disclose its innermost secret only unsteadily and uncertainly.... I know how indescribable it is and how quickly it passes away.... Would that I could and might express it, at least indicate it, without having to desecrate it.

Schleiermacher's understanding of language is more complex than this summary might indicate. He understood, for example, that language is not an individual matter but a product of culture. This means that expressions and interpretations of religious experience will necessarily vary from culture to culture and from person to person. In this sense, he anticipated some critical twentieth-century developments in the philosophy of language. But for purposes of understanding Schleiermacher's impact on liberal theology, the critical point is that language always follows experience. This means that all forms of religious language, whether uttered in song, sermon, or doctrine, are secondary. They derive from and are therefore subordinate to religious experience. This view affects our understanding of the role of theology. Schleiermacher put it this way in the introduction to his own systematic theology:

> Christian doctrines are accounts of the Christian religious affections set forth in speech.... The doctrines in all their forms have their ultimate ground so exclusively in the emo-

tions of the religious self-consciousness, that where these do not exist the doctrines cannot arise.

In other words, for Schleiermacher, theology might be defined as "reflection upon and clarification of believing experience."

Schleiermacher's view has had a lasting impact on liberal theology. Consider William James' *The Varieties of Religious Experience*, perhaps the most influential treatment of the topic during the twentieth century. Here James offered his famous definition of religion:

> Religion, therefore, as I now ask you arbitrarily to take it, shall mean for us the feelings, acts and experiences of individual men in their solitude, so far as they apprehend themselves to stand in relation to whatever they may consider the divine.

This definition clearly echoes Schleiermacher in its emphasis on individual experience, though it is more open-ended about the ways in which the content of that experience might be perceived. For James, a sense of connection with something beyond ourselves forms the basis of human religious experience. We may be aware, for example, of "a feeling of objective presence, a perception of what we may call 'something there.'" In another well-known passage toward the end of the book, James summarized the "essence" of the religious experience:

> The individual...becomes conscious that [his] higher part is conterminous and continuous with a MORE of the same quality, which is operative in the universe outside of him, and which he can keep in working touch with, and in a fashion get on board of and save himself when all his lower being has gone to pieces in the wreck.

The sense is one of inhabiting an "invisible spiritual environment" in which we feel joined with something larger than ourselves, a mysterious "more."

James followed the basic religious road map drawn by Schleiermacher in several important ways. First, he continued the idea that religion itself is fundamentally about personal inward experience. Indeed, he had even less interest than Schleiermacher in institutional and theological matters:

> Now in these lectures I propose to ignore the institutional branch entirely, to say nothing of the ecclesiastical organization, to consider as little as possible the systematic theology and the ideas about the gods themselves, and to confine myself as far as I can to personal religion pure and simple.

Second, Schleiermacher, like James, understood the basic nature of this inward experience to involve a felt sense of relationship with the divine. Third, James agreed that religious experience is somehow beyond or prior to language. His most direct treatment of this point is found in his discussion of mysticism. While in some sense mysticism might seem a special case, James was clear that "personal religious experience has its root and centre in mystical states of consciousness." And one of the central features of a mystical state is what James called its ineffability:

> The subject of it immediately says that it defies expression, that no adequate report of its contents can be given in words. It follows from this that its quality must be directly experienced; it cannot be imparted or transferred to others. In this peculiarly mystical states are more like states of feeling than like states of intellect. No one can make clear to another who has never had a certain feeling, in what the quality or worth of it consists.

Finally, like Schleiermacher, the priority of religious experience led James to view theology as a second-order activity. "Feelings, acts and experiences" are central, and it is "out of religion" understood in this manner that "theologies, philosophies, and ecclesiastical organizations may secondarily grow." Or as he put it later in the book: "In a world in which no religious feeling had ever existed, ... I doubt whether any philosophic theology could ever have been framed."

For liberal theology in the twentieth century, this experience-based orientation is perhaps best represented by a branch of liberalism known as empirical theology. This is primarily a North American phenomenon, stemming mainly from the pragmatist philosophy of William James and John Dewey. It continues to have many adherents and is a fairly prominent movement within liberal theology today. As its name suggests, experience is the central category in all forms of empirical theology. Most empirical theologians assume the possibility of direct, immediate experience of God. At the same time, they have been concerned with exploring and understanding the nature of what is experienced. In general, empirical theology has emphasized the naturalistic, and even the finite, nature of God. As Nancy Frankenberry writes,

> Empirical theologians have sought to identify an activity operative in the universe and human life that issues in *growth of value*. This growth or progressive integration is regarded as one factor within evolution. It is persistent, but not inevitable, or omnipotent; indeed, it is often reversed or suppressed.... Conceived as finite, God is that factor that makes sense of the ways in which harmony and complexity, patterned order and novel emergents, arise and are sustained in nature generally, as well as in the dim regions of organic evolution and amid the conflicts of historical strife.

Empirical theology, then, is concerned with describing and analyzing the experiential, observable evidence of the unfolding nature of this process. Put in traditional theological terms, its concern is with the way God's work is perceived and manifest in the world.

One of the key early figures of this movement was Henry Nelson Wieman. In his first book, *Religious Experience and Scientific Method*, published in 1926, Wieman laid out the experiential grounding of his theology in strong terms. God, he claimed,

> is an object of immediate experience. Mystical experience of the sort we shall portray... must be scientifically interpreted

if we are to know what God is. If by God we mean the object of such experience, without any further attempt to describe his character, then there can be not the slightest doubt in the world that God exists. For there can be no question about the reality of religious experience.

Wieman was not interested in debating the existence or nonexistence of God. He simply assumed God's existence. But this assumption was not based on philosophical speculation, or logical deduction, or any sort of blind faith that lies beyond the reach of reason. Instead, it arises out of actual human experience.

Wieman's understanding of experience was much broader in scope than the feeling of absolute dependence described by Schleiermacher. For Wieman, mystical religious experience involves an opening of oneself to the widest possible range of sensuous qualities that may be available in the present moment. He described this as a "state of diffusive awareness" such that "one becomes aware of a far larger portion of that totality of immediate experience which constantly flows over one." This view is typical of empirical theologians following Wieman. Here, experience includes not only sensory experience, but also the emotional, volitional, aesthetic, and social dimensions of experience, as well as relations to the natural and social worlds.

Most empirical theologians are concerned with the kinds of knowledge about God that our religious experience gives us. Wieman argued that it immediately generates what he called knowledge by acquaintance. From it, we can know that we have experienced God. But if we want to know something about God, we must acquire knowledge by description, the kind of knowledge we get by scientific inquiry and other forms of systematic reflection. This is what Wieman meant when he said that religious experience "must be scientifically interpreted if we are to know what God is." For Wieman, this is the work of theology. Its central task is to investigate our primary experiences of God and try to discern just what sort of object God is. Wieman's own theological explorations led him to the view that God is simply that reality or power in the world that can transform human life and lead to its highest fulfillment. In his early writings, Wieman often called this a Something, whatever it may be, that has this capacity. Later, he identified this power as existing within a type of communicative process he called creative interchange. However it is labeled, this power is real, it exists within the natural world, and its impact on human existence can be felt and verified through direct experience.

This sort of theological reflection is important work. It is essential if our religious experiences are to be developed in ways that deepen our understanding of God and guide our day-to-day living. But Wieman, like Schleiermacher and James before him, saw this as a secondary activity. Descriptive or conceptual knowledge is less important than direct "knowledge by acquaintance." Wieman was concerned that without direct experiential knowledge, God would be reduced to a mere concept that exists only in the mind. Direct knowledge has priority because it affirms God's reality. Thus God's reality and God's availability to human experience are the central premises of Wieman's empirical theology. Without this, he said, "we have no religion at all."

In his later writing Wieman continued to develop and refine his understanding of God and its implications for our personal and social lives. He also came to recognize the ways in which our religious experience is affected by the concepts we bring to it. In other words, Wieman was increasingly affected by the emerging linguistic turn. In a book written thirty-two years after his first book, he commented on the role played by culture in shaping our religious experience into meaningful forms:

> The mind cannot suddenly take on new forms of appreciative consciousness radically different from those of the prevailing culture because every human mind is shaped by creative communication with associates. While the individual can make his own unique contribution, it is always a contribution, not the sudden creation of a totally new kind of mentality.... Hence, when creativity in the mystic experience breaks through the bounds of these cultural forms, the

new forms cannot depart very far from those of the culture. The institutions, the way of thought, and the perception already established in the society, resist sudden change. Even the mind of the mystic is held in bondage to his culture although he advances somewhat beyond it.

And in his last book, written in 1968, Wieman continued to note that the concepts and categories used to turn our experience into knowledge are themselves "constructs of the human imagination" that precede and help guide our interpretive efforts.

Even in these late works, Wieman continued to affirm the possibility of direct and uninterpreted mystical experience. In other words, he stopped short of the fully linguistic approach we find in much postmodern theology. Throughout his career, Wieman remained committed to the idea that whatever else God may be, God is a reality that can be directly experienced and described. Here Wieman remained a typical, perhaps the prototypical, empirical theologian.

Even among theologians who do not think of themselves as empiricists, the emphasis on experience has continued to be a central feature of much liberal theology. A prominent example is Sallie McFague, who recognizes that the term *experience* is highly problematic. Even so, we are stuck with it, she suggests, "because in its most basic sense experience simply means the act of living." This is too broad a definition to be useful, but it is important to understand where McFague is going with this. First, while experience is an important reference point, she is not using it like Schleiermacher or Wieman as the starting point for her entire theology. She is offering it as part of her proposal for an organic model of the universe, one that recognizes and values both radical diversity and deep interconnectedness. Our awareness and understanding of these relationships, she suggests, turn on the nature of our experience.

Second, for McFague the relevant religious experience is not the inward mystical experience emphasized by Schleiermacher or Wieman. Instead, it is "embodied" experience and precisely the kind of experience that opens us to the organic interdependence of our world:

> Experience is *felt* experience, the experience of bodies at the most elemental level. Experience begins with feelings of hot and cold, hunger and satiety, comfort and pain, the most basic ways in which all creatures live in their environments. We live here also and this basic level connects us in a web of universal experience making possible an ever-widening inclusive sympathy for the pains and pleasures of creatures like and unlike ourselves.

McFague recognizes that human experience is always embodied culturally as well as biologically:

> Even physical reality is experienced differently depending on one's cultural, economic, racial, and gender situation. There is no experience-in-general nor any body-in-general, yet there is experience and there is body, both constructed and both particular.

This means there can be no universal human experience. Yet we are all experiencing beings, and for McFague, our common experience as embodied beings can become the basis for an understanding of reality that takes bodies and their needs seriously. This then becomes the basis for recognizing the divine in other beings as well as for a model of justice.

The Linguistic Turn

Postmodern thought challenges our traditional liberal understanding of religious experience and its relation to language. It would be simplistic to cast this controversy as one involving liberal-modern versus postliberal-postmodern views. Nevertheless, the questions these developments raise for the liberal theological tradition are important and deserve to be taken seriously. In terms of its impact

on our view of religious experience, the most significant development is the so-called *linguistic turn* in the philosophy of language.

The linguistic turn signals the emergence of a new paradigm,
one that challenges the "turn to the subject" that marked modern
philosophy three centuries earlier. This paradigm developed along
two independent lines. One moved through the linguistic philosophy of Ludwig Wittgenstein (1889-1951), the other through the
field of philosophical hermeneutics.

PHILOSOPHY OF LANGUAGE. Wittgenstein emphasized that the
meaning and truth-value of words are determined by their actual
use. Our linguistic practices follow certain conventions or rules,
but the rules have no meaning apart from the social practices, or
language games, in which they are used. For example, there is
nothing inherent in the word *chair* that relates it to the object we
sit on. We know this object as a chair because of our shared cultural usage of this word. The same is true for abstract concepts
such as truth or freedom, even though we may disagree on their
precise meanings. We can have these disagreements precisely because we share a set of historical usages related to these terms.

Our language games always take place within a social context.
It is the shared meanings that make communication through language possible. There can be no private language, no language
whose use is limited to an individual's own experiences. Language
always has public meaning. The criteria for correct use are always
public criteria, established by the practices of the particular language group. Because meaning is created communally, the individual no longer occupies center stage. The individual still
matters, but only as a result of a social process in which meaning
is created intersubjectively, through language. The relevant reference point is now what we might call a collective subject, or as
philosopher Seyla Benhabib puts it, a "social community of actual
language users."

Jürgen Habermas has built on Wittgenstein's work and broad-
ened our understanding of the role of language. Wittgenstein was

concerned with what is often called the grammar of linguistic practice in communities, the rules and social practices that make shared meaning possible. Habermas argues, however, that language involves not simply speech, but "speech-acts." In other words, when we communicate through speech, we are not just making sounds that reflect a set of shared meaning conventions. We are also acting. Habermas calls this the performative function of language.

When we speak, we enter into a three-part relationship with the world. First, we make a claim about something. In this way, we create a relationship with the object of our speech. Second, we express our own intentions or purposes. And third, we establish an interpersonal relationship with the listener. This may be a continuation of an ongoing relationship or it may be entirely new. It may be deep and lasting or shallow and perfunctory. But communication through language is always a relational activity. It requires two or more individuals who normally share not just a common vocabulary but a social context and a basic intention to communicate with and understand each other. We have come a long way from the modern philosophy of the subject, in which internal reflection and autonomous reason define who we are as human selves. In the linguistic paradigm, all of our knowledge and experience are mediated by language.

HERMENEUTICS. When we hear the term *hermeneutics*, we ordinarily think of the problem of interpretation, especially the interpretation of texts. Many books are devoted to fields such as biblical hermeneutics, for example, dealing with methods of interpreting scripture. But in the twentieth century, the field of philosophical hermeneutics began to concern itself with the larger questions of human communication and understanding in general. And these developments have affected the ways in which we think about our own experiences.

One of the central lessons of hermeneutics is that in our efforts to understand the world and our place in it, we are always interpreting. Language, of course, is one of the major tools of our interpretations. And as we have seen, language is a social phenomenon. Another key element is what German philosopher Martin Heidegger (1889-1976) called our preunderstandings, which are supplied by our cultures and become part of our life context. They are always with us even though we may not be conscious of them. They affect how we see and interpret the world. Our entire conscious awareness is filtered through them. This means that "all perception is always already interpretation."

German philosopher Hans Georg Gadamer (1900-2002) narrowed the subject's playing field even more. For Gadamer, understanding takes place within the horizons of "a historically situated, intersubjective lifeworld." And this lifeworld is not purely objective; we are constantly interpreting it and adjusting our understanding of it. Moreover, understanding always occurs through the medium of language, which is itself a product of a particular historical and cultural context. In other words, the subject is always situated both "horizontally in the dimension of language and understanding" and "vertically in the dimension of history and tradition." The result is that the very process of understanding is always intersubjective and contextual, completely undermining the autonomous, self-validating rational subject of modernity. Indeed, we can now see that the very concept of the autonomous rational individual was itself an interpretive lens, the product of a particular historical and cultural situation.

Following these developments in the philosophy of language, the traditional liberal-modern way of understanding the relationship between experience and language was turned upside down. In the linguistic view, we don't first have experiences and then afterward interpret and express them in words. Our experiences are themselves shaped and in a certain sense constructed by the conceptual and symbolic reference points supplied by our cultures, especially language. The liberal Roman Catholic theologian David Tracy puts it this way: "We do not first experience or understand some reality and then find words to name that understanding. We understand in and through the languages available to us." This view leads to a different understanding of both experience and language. Rather than being simply expressive or descriptive, language is now seen as constructive. It helps create the very reality that we describe with it. Tracy continues,

> Language is not an instrument that I can pick up and put down at will; it is always already there, surrounding and invading all I experience, understand, judge, decide, and act upon. I belong to my language far more than it belongs to me.

Postliberal theologian George Lindbeck argues that the postmodern emphasis on the priority of language changes the relationship between the inward and outward dimensions of our experience. Under the liberal-modern understanding, the external aspects of our religion are derived from our inner experiences. But under the postmodern cultural-linguistic understanding, "it is the inner experiences which are viewed as derivative." This means that "there are numberless thoughts we cannot think, sentiments we cannot have, and realities we cannot perceive unless we learn to use the appropriate symbol systems." Or, as theologian Paul Lakeland puts it, "what can be said lays down the boundaries of what can be thought."

The postmodern emphasis on the role of symbols, including language, builds on important developments in other fields. Philosopher Susanne K. Langer, whose groundbreaking studies of symbolism have been highly influential, makes this important point:

> Symbolism is the recognized key to that mental life which is characteristically human and above the level of sheer animality. Symbol and meaning make man's world, far more than sensation.

Cultural anthropologist Clifford Geertz, building on the work of Langer and others, sees culture itself as a complex set of overlapping symbol systems:

> The term "culture"…denotes an historically transmitted pattern of meanings embodied in symbols, a system of inherited conceptions expressed in symbolic forms by means of which [human beings] communicate, perpetuate, and develop their knowledge about and attitudes toward life.

These insights are profoundly important for our understanding of ourselves as experiencing beings. Geertz points out that our brains and central nervous systems evolved in constant interaction with our cultures and with the symbol systems and meaning-making structures they provide, including language. This means that our "symbols are thus not mere expressions, instrumentalities, or correlates of our biological, psychological, and social existence; they are prerequisites of it." Language, in other words, is a condition of our psychological and social existence as fully human beings.

Theologian Gordon Kaufman argues that human subjective experience is largely made possible by language. We commonly think of subjective phenomena such as feelings, desires, hopes, and so on, as occurring in some sort of interior personal space. But Kaufman, citing both Geertz and Wittgenstein, argues that the experiences we normally think of as inner or subjective cannot be brought to conscious awareness without the frame of reference provided by language. Personal pronouns such as "I" and "me" are linguistic reference points that enable us to distinguish ourselves from other objects. They also make it possible for us to be aware of ourselves as experiencing subjects. By the same token, we learn to associate certain subjective feelings and experiences with the "I," and we often describe these experiences with metaphors of "inwardness" and the like. But language provides us with patterns of meaning that allow us to locate and make sense of these experiences. Kaufman sums up:

Human subjectivity remains largely inchoate until, in the course of the development of a person from infancy through childhood into maturity, it is given a specific shape and character by the language and culture and patterns of social interaction which are internalized as the self is created.

Language, in other words, is "the fundamental ordering principle of experience."

One of the crucial implications of this linguistic perspective is that there is no such thing as raw or pure or uninterpreted experience. All of the perceptions, activities, thoughts, wonderings, pains, pleasures, and other events of our daily lives are always experienced in terms of the conceptual categories and linguistic structures supplied by our cultures. As Kaufman suggests, this is true for ordinary experiences, such as whether a particular kind of food is appealing or nauseating; for moral questions, such as whether a baby girl is to be valued as highly as a boy; and for "ultimate" questions, such as how we respond to our own finitude or whether we experience the universe as friendly or unfriendly. These occasions never occur in a vacuum; our conceptual and cultural frames of reference inevitably affect the experiences themselves. Experience is not first had and then interpreted; it is always already interpreted.

This principle has obvious implications for religious claims. Most importantly, it challenges any claim to direct experience of God or ultimate reality. Liberal Roman Catholic theologian Francis Schüssler Fiorenza puts it this way:

> When persons claim to have had an experience of God, this experience is not a pure experience, but is an experience mediated through the paradigms of cultural religious history as to what is the meaning of God and what counts as an experience of that meaning.

It is not that the experience is illusory; none of the theologians or philosophers who adopt this position denies the existence of experiences of this type. The problem comes when they are taken to be evidential or to justify claims about the nature of the perceived object of the experience. We could not understand these experiences as religious unless we already had available the concept of religion and some reference points for understanding what makes a particular type of experience count as religious. By the same token, we could not understand a particular experience as being of God unless we first had available to us the linguistic symbol *God*, as well as supporting concepts or images of God to draw on. In other words, as Wayne Proudfoot notes, "religious experience cannot be identified without reference to concepts, beliefs, grammatical rules, and practices" supplied by our cultures and our languages. This means that "religious language is not only the expressive, receptive medium Schleiermacher takes it to be. It also plays a very active and formative role in religious experience."

These postmodern developments force us to reevaluate the central claims of liberal theology as represented by Schleiermacher, James, and others. We may take as an example Schleiermacher's elaboration of his central claim that the "essence of piety" is a "feeling of absolute dependence":

> God is given to us in feeling in an original way; and if we speak of an original revelation of God to man or in man, the meaning will always be just this, that, along with the absolute dependence which characterizes not only man but all temporal existence, there is given to man also the immediate self-consciousness of it, which becomes a consciousness of God.

Notice that Schleiermacher has already moved here from the experience of God into a theological interpretation of that experience. Yet in the postmodern view, we see that Schleiermacher's own sophisticated understanding of these concepts, as well as his life experiences in the Lutheran church and the German culture, are already at work in the experiences themselves. In other words, Schleiermacher could perceive his experience to be one of absolute dependence on God only because he already had clear ideas about what *God*, *absolute*, and *dependence* mean. Proudfoot, commenting on Schleiermacher's treatment of religious experience, notes that

> Concepts, beliefs, and practices are assumed by the descriptions he offers and the instructions he gives for identifying the religious moment in experience.... These are not simple inner states identifiable by acquaintance, as Schleiermacher and others suggest. Such moments of experience are clearly dependent on the availability of particular concepts, beliefs, and practices.

We can make the same point by examining some of the many examples used by James. One of the things that makes James's treatment of religious experience so effective is his brilliant reporting on the critical experiences of so many people, both historical and contemporary. From the postmodern view, this is also the source of the problem. One of James's correspondents reported, for example, "By this divine light...I saw that...I had many other evils to put away and to cease from...[which]...by the light of Christ were made manifest to me." Another states, "Feeling my own weakness, and having entirely given up my own will, I repaired to God like a man in distress who had no more resources. He answered,...[and] my heart no longer felt any difficulty."

At first glance, these reports seem to be descriptions of unique, personal religious experiences. But in their telling, they make use of several preexisting symbols and cognitive categories that derive their meaning through the larger culture, without which the reports would make no sense. These include *divine, evil, Christ, God,* and *will*. Moreover, these symbols represent sophisticated concepts that stand in complex relationships with each other and make sense only in light of meanings and interpretations supplied by the tradition within which they emerged, in this case Christianity. In other words, these experiences, while profound and perhaps life-changing, were not preinterpretive or prelinguistic. They could not have been perceived in this way— they could not have been experienced as these experiences—

unless the possibility of this particular interpretation was already available.

KAUFMAN'S CRITIQUE. Gordon Kaufman offers a different kind of challenge to experience-based theology. To begin, Kaufman disagrees that God is directly available to human experience. God is not like the tables and chairs and other physical objects of our experience. Instead, *God* is the term we use to name the creative cosmic and evolutionary forces that ground and sustain everything that exists. Our ideas about God are our own imaginative constructions, which we form using mental concepts together with various sets of metaphors and images. This does not mean there is no reality behind the metaphors. The evolutionary and historical processes that create and sustain us and our world are real, as is the ultimate mystery out of which they emerged. But it does mean that "God is not an object immediately available to human beings, to be perceived, examined, described, interpreted." For Kaufman, our felt experiences of personal relationship with God "have their real grounding in our actual interpersonal relations on the human level," and it is "through these relationships that we will come to realize whatever personal relation with God ... is possible for us."

At one level, Kaufman simply has a different understanding of God than that of most empirical theologians. Yet his claim that God is not an object of direct experience raises a series of critical challenges for any experienced-based approach. One challenge is methodological. For Kaufman, experience is not an appropriate starting point for theology. To begin, there is the problematic nature of the concept of experience. Many types of human experience have been used as bases for theological reflection. Liberation theology, for example, begins with the social experience of oppression rather than with personal mystical experience. Another problem is that even if we could agree on a proper experiential starting point, there is nothing inherent in that experience that tells us how to move on to the next step. "Without additional guiding principles, methods of procedure, and criteria of judgment (themselves not directly supplied by experience), it would be impossible to know how to proceed in moving from 'experience' to theology." In other words, "religious experience" is simply too vague a concept to be useful as the primary grounding for theological reflection.

Interestingly, a similar insight has been offered by Nancy Frankenberry, one of today's leading advocates for empirical theology and empirical philosophy of religion. While not citing Kaufman, she agrees that the term *experience* has held a variety of different and often inconsistent meanings over the years. As a result, "the appeal to experience in religion usually has raised more problems than it has solved." Frankenberry recognizes that this raises methodological difficulties:

> In general, empirical theology has found that the appeal to experience is methodologically legitimate only to the extent that it is coupled with and refers to an interconnected set of interpretations about what constitutes the nature, scope, and limits of experience. It forfeits legitimacy if it is advanced as a simple appeal to an isolated fact or set of facts. Least credible is any introspective appeal to "religious experience" understood individualistically.

This approach amounts to a rejection of the inner experience held up by Schleiermacher and James. Yet unlike Kaufman, it is clear that Frankenberry and other empirical theologians insist that, with appropriate caution, religious experience may still hold center stage in theology.

Another challenge relates to the kinds of knowledge or truth claims we can derive from our religious experience. At the most basic level, we can ask, "How do we know that our experience is really an experience of God?" This question is more problematic in light of the postmodern insight that our experiences always involve interpretation. Who is to say whose interpretation is correct? From a theological perspective, the problem is not with the experience itself. For Kaufman, at least, the problem arises when theological assertions, especially claims about the nature of God, are made and justified by "a more or less straightforward 'reading off' of data given directly and immediately" in experience. The idea that we can have direct access to ultimate reality is problematic enough. It is even more so when we claim to acquire specific knowledge from such an encounter.

Kaufman worries that we are in danger of "reifying" our religious metaphors when we make these kinds of strong claims. We reify an idea when we inappropriately turn it into a thing. For example, we may take symbols such as *lord* or *father* to mean that God is literally a lord or a father, rather than as metaphors. As Kaufman puts it,

> The strong conviction that one is dealing with what is *really the case* can all too easily allow (or lead to)...our taking them as concrete *realities* rather than recognizing them to be the imaginative constructs which they in fact always are.

This sort of conviction can also lead to claims that we have privileged access to God's will in the world. And as we know only too well, conflicting claims of this sort can easily lead to conflict, sometimes war. For Kaufman, the way to avoid this problem is to realize that in theology, we are always dealing with matters that are beyond our comprehension, that we are confronted with ultimate mystery. He advocates using the term *mystery* rather than *reality* to remind us of this problem and to help us maintain an appropriate religious humility.

Before we leave Kaufman's critique, several additional observations are in order. First, this challenge comes from within the liberal tradition, not from without. Kaufman is regarded as one of the leading liberal theologians of our time. This makes his critique especially important for liberal theology.

Second, Kaufman is not saying that human experience can never lead to knowledge. Obviously we acquire certain types of knowledge from the ordinary experiences of our daily lives, although in the postmodern way of looking at it, we must be aware that this knowledge is filtered through the interpretive lenses supplied by our culture. More than this, the idea of "embodied knowing" has become an important feature in some feminist and liberation theologies. This approach emphasizes the idea that we are embodied beings and that the body—not simply the spirit or intellect—needs to become a central reference point in our theological reflection. As Sallie McFague says, an embodiment theology can move us

> toward a more inclusive sense of justice for the needs of *all* (embodied) human beings. In an embodiment ethic, hungry, homeless, or naked human beings have priority over the spiritual needs of the well-fed, well-housed, well-clothed sisters and brothers.

Kaufman would not disagree with this; his own theological understanding of human beings is rooted in the reality that we are embodied beings.

Kaufman's critique is not intended as a broadside attack on all empirical modes of doing theology. Many aspects of lived human experience are appropriate subjects for theological reflection. We might, for example, take a psychological approach and examine our ways of apprehending and interpreting the types of experience we call religious. Or we might draw on the social sciences and critically examine a particular group's experience of oppression in light of certain religious norms and symbols. This has been one of the central tasks of liberation theology. Kaufman even suggests there might be "an empirical theology attentive to the mysteries of existence," perhaps in conversation with physics or other natural sciences. All of these forms of experience-based theological inquiry are perfectly acceptable as long as their "thoroughly constructive character" is recognized. In the end, Kaufman's critique stands as a warning against unjustified overreaching when we make claims of knowledge based solely on a particular form of experience.

CAUTIONARY NOTES. The postmodern linguistic challenge to the primacy of experience in liberal theology has not escaped challenges of its own. Nancy Frankenberry warns that a kind of relativism is inherent in the linguistic turn that could lead to new forms of *fideism*, or the belief that religious truth is purely a matter of faith—and that reason plays no role at all. In this view, one's religious convictions cannot be defended or justified by any form of evidence or rational argument. Historically, fideism represents a perspective that is the polar opposite of liberalism. In practice, it can lead to an intellectual isolationism that avoids interaction with the sciences and other forms of modern knowledge. The connection between fideism and postmodern thought is found in Wittgenstein's concept of "language games."

Wittgenstein proposed that each social group and each field of knowledge operates within the rules of its own language game. These language games are beyond justification. They are simply there, supplying the rules of discourse for a particular group. Each form of discourse has its own customs and practices, including its own criteria of rationality and coherence. This means that no mode of discourse or particular language game can be criticized from the perspective of any other. Just as we cannot justifiably criticize the game of baseball by applying the rules of chess, so we cannot criticize religion by applying the laws of physics (or vice versa). By the same token, because these language games are linked to specific cultures, there are no universal criteria we can apply. Science, religion, art, politics, and so on live within their own spheres and speak their own languages, which are often unintelligible to outsiders.

Frankenberry has argued strongly against following the linguistic turn too far down this fideist path in theology. Something important is lost when religious groups refuse to interact with other groups or with other dimensions of the larger culture. In fact, complete isolation is not really possible. Ironically, on postmodern grounds themselves, fideistic belief systems are products of certain cultural influences and always exist within specific cultural contexts. Beyond this, as Frankenberry reminds us, using the linguistic turn to justify this isolationism "is nothing other than an ideological shelter for protecting religious beliefs from examination, refutation, or revision." In the end, this approach simply reinforces a hard dogmatism and leads to "roughly the same conservative attitudes that also characterize evangelical Christianity." Frankenberry's warning seems to be that liberal theology, by overemphasizing the priority of language, could end up undercutting one of its basic characteristics: its openness to the sciences and adaptability to the larger culture.

A second critique emerges out of Sallie McFague's theological emphasis on embodied experience. McFague rejects the view that the self and its experiences are always mediated by language. For McFague, experience is always embodied, "*felt* experience, the experience of bodies at the most elemental level." She continues,

> Embodied experience links the cries of a hungry child and a wounded animal, the exhilaration we feel at the sight of a magnificent sunset and the soothing touch of a hand on a painful sore. Through our bodies, in their agonies and ecstasies that lie behind and beyond all linguistic expression, we are bound into a network of relations with our natural environment and experience ourselves as bodies with other bodies. Whatever else experience means, it includes bodily experience as a primordial reality, uniting us in ever-widening concentric circles with the entire planet in all its diverse, rich forms of embodiment.

McFague is concerned that too great an emphasis on the role of language in human experience can artificially separate us from other creatures. We can come to see our human situation as qualitatively different, and this can block our ability to sense our deep, bodily interconnectedness with the rest of the natural world:

> That line of demarcation is neither justified in relation to other animals (who do have forms of communication) nor absolute in relation to ourselves (we do experience more

than we can express in language—otherwise, why are poets and mystics dissatisfied with their efforts at expressing their experiences?).

In a sense, of course, putting it this way simply begs the question. But McFague's concern that human experience not be reduced to language is clear enough.

This is not to say that McFague is unconcerned with the role of religious language. Throughout most of her career, religious language, especially the metaphors we use to name our images of God, has been one of her central concerns. Like most liberals, she insists that all language of God is metaphorical. Moreover, the kinds of metaphors we use make a difference not only in our understanding of God but more importantly in the way we live our lives. Though she doesn't say this directly, her analysis of metaphor suggests that the language we use to refer to God may have a direct effect on the way we experience God—as loving and supportive, angry and judgmental, and so on. Our language matters.

McFague is also enough of a postmodernist to recognize that our experience, including our experience of God, is always interpreted:

> We are always involved in a hermeneutical spiral that has no clear entrance or exit. We are born into particular circumstances and communities that form us at the most basic levels and interpret our experience for us in ways that we cannot control and, in significant ways, do not even recognize. Yet we also participate in and add to the spiral of interpretation, making claims that our experience is or is not adequately interpreted by these formative communities—and when it is not, advancing novel frameworks that are more persuasive.

This means that our interpretations are always partial and limited. We never get it completely right. Here, McFague continues the central claim of Schleiermacher and James that our language is never adequate to express our experience, though McFague's understanding of the reasons for this inadequacy are different. The important point is that even though our experiences are always interpreted, they are real. And they occur in at least some sense prior to any interpretation we bring to them. Our metaphors point to something real. In other words, unlike some liberal theologians today, McFague has followed the linguistic turn only part of the way.

Integrating Language and Experience

The liberal-modern and the postliberal-postmodern approaches are in a sense mirror images. Both view the relationship between religious experience and language as essentially linear; the difference is in their order. For the modernist, religious experience happens first, followed by interpretation and then communication in language. For the postmodernist, it is the other way around: Our conceptual and linguistic categories shape the nature of the experience we have. Both perspectives recognize that language and experience are interconnected, yet neither goes far in helping us understand the nature of the connection.

Recently, some theologians in both the liberal and postliberal camps have begun to move away from these polar views. Gordon Kaufman, for example, notes that we continually live our lives while simultaneously trying to make sense of them. This means that experience and meaning continuously affect and reinforce one another. By the same token, the relationship between experience and language is dialectical:

> Experience is always in this way dialectically interconnected with our reflection on it and our reconstruction of it. We take in the events of life and the objects of experience in terms of concepts and categories inherited from our culture, even though all the while we are actively participating in the remodeling and remaking of these very categories so they will better fit that experience.

George Lindbeck also recognizes that things are not quite as simple as they might appear. Because he understands religion itself to be a "cultural-linguistic" phenomenon, he sometimes speaks of the relationship between religion and experience rather than between language and experience, but he is getting at the same problem. Thus, he notes that "the relation of religion and experience...is not unilateral but dialectical....The causality is reciprocal." Lindbeck comes down in basically the same place as Kaufman on this point. At the same time, he cannot quite let go of his linguistic perspective. He continues to insist that even though the relationship between the internal and external dimensions is mutual, the external or cultural factors, including language, "can be viewed as the leading partners."

In a recent book that explores the theological implications of these questions, Roman Catholic theologian Thomas Kelly, drawing on the work of philosopher George Steiner, concludes that "to understand either language or 'experience,' a mutuality in the relation between them and not a priority in conditioning must be emphasized." He then applies this insight to his concern for the meaning of doctrine: "Christian doctrine performs both constructive and descriptive functions and clarifies the relationship between 'experience' and 'language' as dialectical." In other words, "the choice is not an either/or but a careful and nuanced both/and."

This dialectical approach to the relationship between language and experience goes a long way toward clarifying our understanding. It acknowledges the insights of the postmodern linguistic perspective while not completely abandoning the experiential perspective of the liberal-modern view. Yet the dialectical approach continues to treat language and religious experience as separate realities—mutual and interdependent, but nevertheless distinct. I believe there is more promise in a broader and more organic approach, one that treats language and other cultural influences as part of experience.

Ironically, the postmodern challenge has opened the door to a more nuanced understanding of the relationship between religious experience and language. The liberal-modern view defines religious experience too narrowly, isolating it from its surrounding context. The postmodern view, while offering a helpful corrective, all but reduces experience to language and thereby devalues its importance for religious life. Neither view is very satisfying. A more relational approach would give up the stale argument about which element has priority. Let us begin by recognizing that these cannot really be separated.

Human experience—religious or otherwise—always involves a complex process of mutual communicative exchange between the individual and the surrounding environment. Both the individual and the environment bring something to the exchange, and both are affected by it. Much of what the individual brings is provided in the first instance by the culture. Yet each individual also brings distinct elements and possibilities. In human beings, language develops simultaneously with biological functions such as brain development and social functions such as communication and socialization. These processes are complex and interrelated at the deepest level. The human organism's experiences include affective and bodily responses as well as cognitive and linguistic ones. In particular experiences, one or another of these may be felt as dominant. We may, for example, respond to a critical life situation with a particular emotional or physical reaction such as fear or illness. Or we may try to make sense of our experience in some intellectual way. Whichever reaction seems dominant, they are going on simultaneously. We make meaning as much through our emotions as through our cognitions.

Moreover, human experience cannot be neatly separated into discrete events or distinct experiences. It is, to use William James's metaphor, more like a stream. While we may perceive our own experience in more or less identifiable episodes, each experiential moment is linked to what precedes it and what follows it, as well as to the context or environment in which it occurs. None of our experiences stands alone. If we humans are truly social beings, then our "personal" experience is not something we have as isolated individuals. The context itself becomes part of the experience and includes not only the evolutionary and environmental realities that make us the embodied biological creatures we are, but also the cultural and social realities that make us the historical beings we also are. These cultural realities include basic value patterns, meaning-making structures (including our religious traditions), and of course language.

The postmodern critique that the kinds of mystical experiences described by Schleiermacher and James are shaped by the meaning-making structures already available to us is correct as far as it goes. For example, I agree that I cannot have what I perceive as an awe-filled experience of God unless I already have the idea of God and the word *God* available to me. But this is only part of the story. What I bring to the experience includes not only the language and concepts supplied by my culture, but my biochemical capacity for affective responses like awe (or wonder, joy, fear, etc.). And these capacities are embodied as well as enculturated. I may be predisposed by childhood learning to look out at the stars and see God and to interpret the accompanying emotional response positively as one of joy or well-being. But the response is real; I feel it in my bones. Something happens to me bodily as well as cognitively. And as I grow and learn, I may come to understand—and perhaps even to feel—the experience in a different way. But it seems overly simplistic to say either that the experience itself is completely independent or that it is completely determined by the cultural factors. Instead, these factors are part of what I necessarily bring to the experience. In this sense, they become part of the experience.

This approach deserves far more analysis than we can give it here. The goal has been to show how the traditional liberal understanding of religious experience, and in turn the role of theology and religious language, is called into question by these postmodern developments. But we need not be afraid of these ideas. Instead, we can use them to help nudge us toward a more nuanced and organic understanding. This opening can lead us as well toward a richer appreciation of our religious language and our religious experience and perhaps even toward richer experiences themselves.

Liberation Theology

RELIGIOUS LIBERALS OFTEN RESPOND positively to liberation theology when they first encounter it. This makes sense because liberation theology is concerned with many of the things liberals are also concerned with, such as overcoming oppression and working for justice in the world. Religious liberals tend to see themselves as justice-seeking people, and liberation theology offers a framework for expressing this goal in theological terms. What is often difficult for liberals to see is that liberation theology is not friendly to liberal theology. Liberation theology begins with different religious assumptions and uses different methods of theological analysis. It is not part of the liberal theological tradition. Instead, it operates as a profound critique of liberal theology.

The liberation critique of liberalism can be placed in sharper relief if we recall the tension in liberal theology around its relationship to social justice. Liberalism's simultaneous commitments to cultural mediation and cultural critique can lead to overly cautious religious stances, which can blunt the edge of liberal social witness. Taken seriously, liberation theology's challenge can help us gain deeper insights into some underlying tendencies that often interfere with liberalism's own best impulses. The importance of the liberation perspective is captured in Cornel West's assessment:

> Liberation theologies are the principal forms of Christian prophetic thought and action in our contemporary age. They present the ways of life and struggle of Christians around the world who have convinced the remnants of the church to open its eyes to human misery and oppose socio-economic systems and political structures that perpetuate such misery.... Liberation theologies are the predominant forms of critical consciousness with the Christian church that respond to the dangers of class, racial and sexual privilege and project the possibility of class, racial and sexual equality.

Liberation theology begins with three commitments that set it apart from liberal theology. First, it presupposes a committed and active Christian faith, which is the source of much of liberation theology's power. Religious liberals, on the other hand, often approach religious faith with caution or skepticism, a test-the-waters attitude that can lead to thin religious commitments. This is not so of the religious commitment that underlies liberation theology. Theological reflection is not done in order to justify faith or rationally to explain it; faith is assumed to exist already. Liberation theology is impatient with discussions about religious belief or doctrine that remain at the academic level, including, for example, theoretical arguments about the existence of God. Instead, religious belief and theological analysis must be linked to concrete historical realities. Otherwise, doctrines and truth claims become

> nothing more than empty abstractions that compose a dogmatic whole without content. Liberation theology's problem is not to deny these beliefs, but to question their significance. Therefore, its question is not 'Does God exist?' but 'Where is God present?' and 'How does God act?'. The point of departure for liberation theology is, then, the question of the concrete and historical place in which God reveals (it)self.

As Brazilian liberation theologian Clodovis Boff puts it, "It is impossible to do a theology of liberation without starting from the 'deposit' of faith," whether or not that faith has been articulated in specific theological doctrines. Second, this faith is expressed in a sustained, living commitment to the process of liberation. Its specific focus is on overcoming oppression, and it is often expressed in terms of a "preferential option for the poor." In other words, liberation theology affirms the existence and redemptive activity of a personal God who acts in history on behalf of the poor and oppressed. As Leonardo and Clodovis Boff put it, "The living God takes sides with the oppressed against the pharaohs of this world." The faith commitment to overcoming oppression is rooted in this understanding of God. It is liberation theology's answer to the question: "What is ultimate in Christian faith?"

The "option for the poor" is easily misunderstood. Liberals are often uncomfortable with a God who takes sides. They like to think of God as neutral, the God of everyone, saint and sinner, rich and poor alike. Liberation theologians, however, say that the liberal discomfort with a God who takes sides reflects the comfortable middle-class perspective of most religious liberals. A preference for neutrality often indicates a position of relative power or privilege. Moreover, Peruvian Catholic priest and theologian Gustavo Gutiérrez, considered the father of Latin American liberation theology, points out that the concept of divine preference does not imply exclusivity. Liberation theology has always "insisted on the importance of maintaining both the universality of God's love and the divine predilection for 'history's last.'" In other words, the poor are God's special focus but not God's only concern.

At a deeper level, many liberals are uncomfortable with any concept of a personal God, including related ideas such as divine purpose. This seems to be incompatible with a scientific worldview, and so they find it hard to relate to the biblical God of liberation theology. Liberation theology does not always use personalistic conceptions of God, but even here the metaphor of

God's option for the poor remains liberation theology's central organizing principle:

> The liberation of the poor [is] that part of the content of theology around which all of theology can be organized—all questions of who God and Christ are, what grace and sin are, what the church and society are, what love and hope are, and so on.

By the same token, the symbol of the kingdom or reign of God takes on central importance. Liberation theology asks what a world organized according to God's justice would look like and answers,

> The Reign of God will be a reign of justice, a world organized in service of the life of those who had been victims, a world that will tear up death and oppression by the roots.... Perhaps we might simply say that the Reign of God is a world, a society, that makes life and dignity possible for the poor.

This theme becomes both a symbol of ultimate hope and a reference point for critiquing existing social structures.

When liberation theologians refer to the poor, they are speaking about social structures, not about individuals. "By 'poor' we do not really mean the poor individual who knocks on the door asking for alms. We mean a collective poor, ... [the] mass of the socially and historically oppressed [that] makes up the poor as a social phenomenon." Jesuit theologian Jon Sobrino, who has lived and worked in El Salvador most of his life, explains that the concept of the poor

> denotes a concrete, historical reality: it means those for whom life is a harsh burden for historical—economic and social—reasons.... The poor are a collective reality; they are poor peoples, or poor as a people. The poor are a historical reality; they are poor not mainly for natural reasons, but historical ones—poor because of injustice.

To say that God has a preference for the poor in this sense is to say, at a minimum, that situations of structural poverty and oppression are unjust. These realities are contrary to the kingdom or reign of God as a reign of justice.

Liberation theology's third starting point is that its theological dialogue partners, or interlocutors, are the poor themselves. Again, this is a major difference from modern liberal theology. Historically, liberal theology's orientation has been toward Schleiermacher's "cultured despisers of religion," or as theologian Harvey Cox puts it, the "sophisticated skepticism of the educated classes." Its central concern has been the possibility and nature of religious belief in a modern scientific age. Liberation theology's focus, in contrast, is not on the difficulty of belief, but on the difficulties of life itself—not on religion's "cultured despisers," but on the culture's "despised Others":

> Liberation theology begins not with the discovery of unbelief, skepticism, but with the discovery of the "absent ones of history," the despised Others. Its interlocutor is not the unbeliever but the hungry person, not the one who questions God, but the one whose carnality and survival is *the* question. While European theologies look at history through the prism of progress/modernization and atheism/theism, liberation theologies look at history from its "underside" through the prisms of oppression/liberation and idolatry/God of life.

Liberation theology's starting point is not the coherence of religion and science or the intellectual curiosity or faith crises of educated believers, but the actual, lived experience of oppression and suffering in the world.

Analysis of Poverty

Analyzing the causes of poverty and oppression is often said to be the first formal step in liberation theology's methodology. In this process, liberation theologians use the social sciences and other analytical tools to undertake a sophisticated inquiry into the root causes of oppression. They engage in procedures that have always been part of the liberal theological method, namely drawing on other academic disciplines and cultural sources as a resource for theology. This kind of social analysis was one of the key elements of the social gospel movement a century ago, for example. So in a sense this approach fits right into the traditional liberal framework.

However, there are important differences relating to the kinds of social analysis liberation theologians do and the types of explanations they find persuasive. Liberation theologians and other commentators have traditionally distinguished three approaches to the analysis of poverty: the conservative, the liberal, and the liberationist. Conservatives tend to see poverty as the result of individual moral failures of the poor themselves. This view is rooted in New England Puritanism and reflects the American mythology of rugged individualism and the so-called Protestant work ethic. Its ethic of self-help leads to social policies that deny or minimize most forms of social assistance. "God helps those who help themselves" might be said to be its theological motto. Its angle of vision is that of the market. The conservative approach has historically been the dominant view in public policy responses to poverty in the United States. Liberation theology rejects this view outright because it not only leaves the dominant system in place, it assumes that the dominant system is working just fine. But the mere existence of widespread poverty and suffering amid enormous concentrations of wealth belies this assumption.

Liberals locate the causes of poverty in social circumstances rather than in the moral failings of the poor. The proper response from the liberal perspective is to create programs and services for those in need. This appears to be a social response, but at a deeper level it remains focused primarily on individuals. The liberal premise is that those who are poor can overcome their condition if they have the right education and opportunities. The liberal goal is to level the playing field and make the system work better for those who have been disadvantaged. This is a corrective, reform-oriented approach. It arises out of an ethic of service, and its most prominent religious expression is in mission work and other forms of hands-on social action.

This service ethic is reflected in the emphasis on social ethics in liberal Protestantism and in the tradition of social teachings and "works of mercy" in Roman Catholicism. Liberal social programs offer a periodic corrective to the harshest consequences of the conservative approach, and liberal religious social outreach helps alleviate some suffering. But liberation theologians reject the liberal approach as fundamentally inadequate. Much has been written on the failure of development programs in Latin America, for example, and Cornel West has spoken of "the impotency of liberalism in the face of structural unemployment and class inequality" in our own society. In the long run, the liberal approach does not work because it leaves the basic social structure in place. From the liberation perspective, the social structure itself is the problem.

Liberationists offer a radical alternative. They see poverty as the inevitable consequence of modern society's economic organization. This perspective focuses on the poor as a social class, not on individuals. Thus, poverty is often referred to as a form of "institutionalized violence." By the same token, the oppression of women and people of color is seen in terms of deep-seated structures of patriarchy and racism rather than as the result of personal bigotry. In their analyses of poverty, liberation theologians address the structural and systemic causes of oppression. Structural analysis also uncovers the overlapping nature of oppressions, such as the concentration of poverty among women and persons of color in the United States. The underlying ethic is neither self-help nor service, but liberation. From the liberation perspective, overcoming these forms of oppression will take more than new social programs and the good will of the middle class; it will take a radical realignment of the social and economic order.

Liberation theology's understanding of poverty has an important theological dimension. Poverty does not signify merely the absence of material well-being, it also signals the absence of true mutuality between human beings and in turn the absence of God. As Franz Hinkelhammert, a German exile in Chile, explains, the liberation of the poor cannot be achieved by those who see the poor as objects. This is an implicit critique of many liberal social programs, but it is also a theological point:

> Without mutual acknowledgment between subjects, in which poverty becomes the negation of the acknowledgment, there is no option for the poor. Human subjects cannot recognize each other without recognizing themselves as corporeal, natural, and needed beings. Poverty is a living negation of this acknowledgment. From liberation theologians' point of view, human beings cannot liberate themselves without a mutual acknowledgment between subjects.

At one level this is a question of human relationships, but it is also about the divine-human relationship. For liberation theology, "God is present wherever this acknowledgement [between subjects] occurs." But the existence of poverty and oppression

> demonstrates a human relationship bereft of God. The existence of the poor attests to the existence of a Godless society, whether one explicitly believes in God or not. This absence of God is present wherever someone is crying out. The absence of God is present in the poor person. The poor are the presence of the absence of God.

This is what makes liberation theology's analysis of poverty simultaneously sociological and theological. It also points to another difference from liberal theology: "The presence of God is no longer an internal emotion, but rather is transformed into praxis (orthopraxis). Its criteria lie in actual reality.... God's presence is a doing, a praxis." Praxis refers to the actual practice of one's faith in service of liberation.

Sources of Theological Authority

Liberation theology examines scripture and tradition with the social analysis of poverty as its reference point. In part this is an aspect of methodology, but liberation theology's method also points to deeper questions, such as: What counts as authority in theological reflection? What are the relevant criteria for truth? Historically, liberals have turned inward for religious authority, relying on their individual experience and reason. Liberation theology takes a very different approach.

Traditional discussions of Christian theology often identify four primary sources of theological reflection: scripture, tradition, reason, and experience. Both liberal and liberation theologies use these, but the emphases are different. Because of its Enlightenment roots, liberal theology has emphasized reason and experience but tended to reject or downplay scripture and tradition. This is not the case in liberation theology. Focusing on these four sources is therefore a useful way of highlighting some important differences.

SCRIPTURE. Most liberation theologies are fundamentally biblical in orientation. They presuppose the authority of scripture and seek to interpret it in ways that support liberation. They do this by reading the Bible from the perspective of the poor and the oppressed. "The liberation theologian goes to the scriptures bearing the whole weight of the problems, sorrows, and hopes of the poor." Two different but complementary interpretive approaches are used in this process. The first is often called a "hermeneutic of suspicion." From this perspective, scripture is examined for ideological distortions that lead to oppression. These distortions are critiqued, and voices and symbols that have been excluded or devalued, such as women's voices, are recovered. At the same time, scripture is read with a "hermeneutic of liberation." This means that stories and symbols that reflect God's liberating action in history, such as the Exodus story, are emphasized.

The liberation approach emphasizes that the social context of the biblical message is an important part of its meaning. Biblical teachings are not just clever stories or abstract sayings. The story of the Exodus is read as an account of God's liberation of a group of enslaved and oppressed peoples. The Prophets' denunciations of injustice were directed at specific rulers and spoke of specific historical situations of a people suffering under this injustice. Jesus' teachings of love and compassion are understood not simply as lessons about individual morality but as directed precisely toward communities suffering extreme economic hardship under Roman imperial occupation. "When it is approached in this way, the biblical text takes on particular relevance in the context of the oppression now being experienced in the Third World." In other words, poor and oppressed people do not simply study the texts for supportive ideas or abstract knowledge. They identify with the situations described and hear their liberating messages of justice as written for them. This is difficult for middle-class liberals to do because scripture tells the story of the poor, not of the middle class.

Both liberals and liberationists use these analytical tools, and both groups number serious biblical scholars among them. As Cox notes, "Liberationists are not fundamentalists in their approach to scripture." But again, the emphasis and even the underlying purpose of biblical study are very different. Liberals tend to look for the meaning of the text in *its* social and historical context; liberationists try to discover what the text means in *their* historical context. This means that the scholars don't get the last word:

> [Liberationists] do not believe that the meaning of a biblical text has been established once the exegetes agree on what it says (as liberal Protestants do), or that its authoritative meaning is decided by the churchly magisterium (as many Catholics hold). Rather, they contend that the most reliable guide to its meaning is seen in what the text means to the poor.

Cox makes the interesting observation that liberal theology ironically "lost the Bible" as a faith resource through the use of the historical-critical method. The Protestant Reformation took the Bible out of the hands of the priests and gave it to the lay people to read for themselves. But critical scholarship

> took it out of the hands of lay people and, instead of returning it to the priests, gave it to the scholars. In effect, among Protestant liberals the hard-won right to read and interpret Scripture on one's own was forfeited to the claim of the scholars that only they were competent to establish what the Bible *really* says.

In a sense, we can say that liberation theology's approach to scripture is an effort to return the Bible to the people.

TRADITION. Liberation theology assumes the authority of tradition. This is also in sharp contrast to liberal theology's tendency to distrust tradition. The liberal assumption has been that looking toward the past is a conservative move and that freedom comes through breaking free of the authoritarian strictures of the past. But liberalism gives up too much by blindly cutting itself off from its own tradition. Turning to the tradition can be a rich resource and need not involve a capitulation to old authoritarian frameworks. The tradition itself must always be reevaluated and critiqued even as it is appropriated, but it remains an important resource, and we disregard it at our peril.

Liberation theology is less ambivalent about tradition. Its grounding in scripture is one dimension of this. In the Roman Catholic context, moreover, liberation theology often turns to the social teachings of the church, itself a long and rich tradition. The church's official social teaching began in 1891 with a papal encyclical entitled *Rerum Novarum*. Among other things, this document argued against class warfare and defended the rights of workers to organize and to receive a just wage. Several such statements on social issues have appeared since then, from the Vatican and other church authorities, right up to the present. In general, these church teachings emphasize the importance of protecting the powerless against the powerful. Many of them address matters of basic economic justice, and some speak to issues of social and political participation as well. One of the most remarkable of these documents is the pastoral letter on the economy issued by the National Conference of Catholic Bishops in 1986, entitled *Economic Justice for All*. Though this document does not identify itself explicitly with liberation theology, it addresses many of the same concerns. In their statement of principal themes, for example, these American bishops note,

> From the Scriptures and church teaching, we learn that the justice of a society is tested by the treatment of the poor.... As followers of Christ, we are challenged to make a fundamental 'option for the poor'—to speak for the voiceless, to defend the defenseless, to assess life styles, policies, and social institutions in terms of their impact on the poor.

While some have criticized this document for not going far enough, its central commitments and basic orientation are in line with the principles of liberation theology.

In the Latin American context, liberation theology's relationship with church authority is somewhat ambivalent. Liberation theologians draw on the tradition of the church's social teachings, though the liberationist perspective is often more radical than the official teachings. This has led to disputes with the church, yet liberation theologians often argue that their theology is consistent with official church teachings. The purpose here is not to address the various controversies that have arisen over the years between liberation theologians and the Vatican, but rather to show that liberation theology understands itself as firmly grounded in its own tradition, even when it is breaking new ground.

Not all liberation theology is Roman Catholic. An important liberation theology arose in the Protestant black church tradition in the United States at about the same time as its Catholic coun-

terpart appeared in Latin America. While these two movements—
and other liberation theologies worldwide—differ in some ways,
their underlying concern is always with liberation from oppression. The central principle in black liberation theology is that God
is involved in the struggle for black liberation from the economic
and social oppressions of white racism. As theologian Dwight N.
Hopkins puts it, black liberation theology's central inquiry is:
"What does it mean to be black and Christian for a people situated
in the midst of American racism and called by God to be fully
human beings?"

Like its Latin American cohort, black liberation theology is
strongly biblical in its orientation. By the same token, it draws on
the experience and social teachings of the black church tradition.
As Baptist minister and professor of Christian social ethics Peter J.
Paris describes it, this tradition is made up of "a constellation of
religious and moral values preserved in institutions and expressed
in speeches, deeds, and actions." The central values of this tradition represent "the primary cause for the emergence of the black
independent churches of the nineteenth century," and they continue to sustain this tradition today. The most prominent denominational groups are the African Methodist Episcopalian Church
and the independent Baptist churches that make up the National
Baptist Convention. Thus, the black church tradition's social
teachings are found in the official reports of the denominational
bodies and the countless sermons, speeches, and other expressions
of individual churches and pastors, as well as in the speeches
and writings of well-known leaders such as W. E. B. DuBois and
Martin Luther King Jr.

These documents offer the churches' perspectives on a range
of social issues, including evolving white attitudes toward African
Americans, the difficulties of African-American participation in
social and political affairs, economic inequalities, and the like. A
recurring theological theme in the denominational reports
throughout the twentieth century is "confidence that God wills
racial justice for human society and that its realization is possible

in this nation." Other important documents in the black church tradition include the statement on black power by the National Committee of Negro Churchmen (now called the National Conference of Black Churchmen) in 1966 and James Forman's famous *Black Manifesto* on economic power in 1969. In the Free Church tradition of most black churches, these documents do not carry the official weight of papal encyclicals. Indeed, some of them have stirred storms of controversy both in the black church and in white liberal Protestant churches. Yet they continue to carry important moral and theological authority in the black theology tradition.

Black liberation theology has built on this tradition while at the same time extending it by developing a new theological framework for addressing black oppression. Similar to the Latin American Catholic experience, black liberation theology has had a mixed reception in the churches themselves. The black churches are not monolithic; as in any denomination or religious tradition, they include a range of theological perspectives. Many are theologically conservative. In a recent study of the black church, C. Eric Lincoln and Lawrence H. Mamiya report that at least two-thirds of African-American ministers in urban churches in the United States have remained unaffected by the black liberation theology movement. Paris goes so far as to suggest that black liberation theology may even be "alien to the black church tradition." Hopkins, however, argues that black liberation theology "works with African-American churches," serving as "a critical conscience of the church's vocation to liberate the poor." Theologian James Cone, the leading figure in the black theology movement, notes that black liberation theology arose "in the context of the struggle of black persons for racial justice." This struggle "was initiated in the black churches," but was more closely associated with the organizations of the civil rights movement. The purpose here is not to assess the reception or influence of black liberation theology in the churches, but to show that, like Latin American liberation theology, it is rooted in tradition while at the same time challenging that tradition in important ways.

EXPERIENCE. Both liberal and liberation theologies take experience as a central starting point. But what counts as the relevant experience is very different. Liberal theology, beginning with Schleiermacher and extending to the present, has focused on the inward mystical experiences of the individual. Liberation theology, in contrast, begins with the lived experience of oppression in the world. This experience is always particular, not universal. That is, liberation theology speaks from the perspective of a particular community's experience of oppression, such as being poor in Latin America or black in white America. It does not try to speak for everyone. This understanding of experience always has a collective or class reference. It never refers simply to individual experiences.

The experiential basis of liberation theology is linked to its faith commitment to overcoming oppression in the world. Its deeply rooted biblical faith is always connected to the experienced reality of poverty and oppression. As theologian Joerg Rieger notes, this means that in contrast to liberal theology, "theology is no longer guided by the experience of the educated middle class alone." Rieger continues,

> While liberal theology rests on the assumption of some basic analogy between humanity and God—herein lies the foundation of the theological authority of the self; theology in dialogue with people on the underside of history must take into account more specifically the experience of brokenness and of separation from God as well.

This is very different from the way the category of experience functions in liberal theology.

REASON. Reason has been an important criterion for liberal religious thought at least since the end of the seventeenth century, when Locke gave it priority over divine revelation. The emphasis on reason during the Enlightenment made it a central feature of liberal theology. Thus, for liberal theology, reason is more than a technique of sound argument or careful analysis; it is a matter of principle. Liberation theology also relies on reason. Liberation theologians, like other theologians, offer extended analysis of theological concepts and careful interpretations of scripture. They also undertake sophisticated and critical analyses of poverty and other social problems and, in doing so, draw on the insights of other disciplines. In this sense, they are very much in line with liberal theology.

Yet there are important differences. Liberal theology has historically been most in dialogue with philosophy and the natural sciences. The key early figures in liberal religious thought, including Locke, Kant, and Schleiermacher, were philosophers as well as theologians. In the nineteenth century, liberal theologians made the first efforts to incorporate Darwinian evolution into Christian theology. And in the twentieth century, liberals continued to explore the theological implications of emerging developments in philosophy and natural science.

Liberation theologians, on the other hand, turn primarily to the social sciences in their work. Their focus is on discovering and overcoming the root causes of social problems such as poverty and oppression, and modern learning in fields such as sociology, economics, and political science offers more resources for this task. This is not to say that liberals do not also do social analysis. Indeed, the first significant theological turn to the social sciences was taken by the liberals involved in the social gospel movement a century ago. A pioneering example is Francis Greenwood Peabody's book *Jesus Christ and the Social Question*, published in 1900, which analyzes the economic and social issues of the emerging industrial order in terms of the gospel message. Throughout the twentieth century, liberals such as James Luther Adams, James Gustafson, and Sharon Welch have been leading figures in theological and social ethics. In this sense, the liberal and liberation traditions share a common concern for theological analysis relating to social justice.

Yet differences remain. When liberals turn to the social sciences in service of their commitment to social justice, they are often in dialogue with the disciplines themselves rather than the people whose lives are most affected. This is not universally the case; many liberals work out of what Welch calls "communities of resistance and solidarity." But many also remain at the level of academic discourse. This kind of analysis makes important contributions to our theological understanding of social issues, but it also highlights an important difference. Liberation theology always remains grounded in the concrete historical reality of the poor themselves. In Latin America, the so-called Christian base communities have provided the popular grounding for liberation theology, and academic theologians often live and minister in impoverished communities. And in the United States, many black theologians remain connected with the African-American community and with developments in black culture.

In liberation theology, reason is never an end in itself. It is always in the service of liberation, and liberation is God's will for those who are oppressed:

> God does not dictate what needs to be done. God's will is to liberate the poor, but the path of freedom has to be searched out. That which ends up being God's will depends on an analysis of reality. Therefore one cannot know God's will without an analysis of reality that never ignores social sciences. And the results of social sciences fall directly upon what, for liberation theology's orthopraxis, is God's will.

Liberation theologians rarely worry about whether their conceptions of God and other theological categories conform to contemporary philosophical and scientific thought. They do not share the liberal preoccupation with making the Christian message credible for educated modern skeptics. Instead, their focus is on how that message is liberating for those on the underside. As a result, liberation theology's criteria are explicitly pragmatic. "Its truth claims emerge when theory meets practice." Theology is true if it is liberating, if it leads to liberating action in the world. The final criterion for liberation theology is not reason, but praxis.

Praxis

Praxis is a key concept in all forms of liberation theology. The term *praxis* (or *eupraxia*) comes from Aristotle, who used it to express a way of living an engaged and ethical public life, or "good action." Aristotle distinguished praxis from two other ways of life, one involving disengaged reflection (*episteme*), and the other focusing on technical or artistic production (*techne*). Marx adopted the notion of praxis to refer to the social grounding of all knowledge. This led to his understanding of truth as a practical question rather than a question of theory and to his emphasis on the relationship between ideology and social structure. By stressing the centrality of praxis, liberation theology aligns itself with these concepts and affirms that its goal is not just conceptual clarity or even a particular form of social organization, but a transformed and liberating way of life.

At the most basic level, in liberation theology *praxis* refers to specific programs for action that emerge from the analysis of poverty in light of biblical and theological principles. This might include what liberals like to call "social action," but it also includes spiritual practices like prayer and bible study on the one hand, and specific involvement in political activity and movements for social change on the other. Praxis involves the actual practice of faith in the service of liberation, that is, in the service of the kingdom of God. It is often expressed in terms of a practice of identification with the poor and oppressed.

At the same time, praxis recognizes that thought is itself a form of action and that both action and thought should continually inform each other. As theologian Rebecca Chopp puts it, "Praxis suggests, then, a bringing together of action and reflection, transformation and understanding. This new marriage of action and reflection depends on accepting human life as fundamentally practical." This means that theological concepts and doctrines emerge out of identification and engagement with the poor in the world and not from the theologian's private reflection. It also means that these theological ideas are then taken back to the world and tested in the court of the people. In liberation theology, there is always "a circular movement from praxis to theoretical reflection and back again to changed praxis."

As Harvey Cox notes, while liberation theology is a practical theology, it is not an "applied theology" in the usual sense of that term. For Cox, this term "suggests a package of ideas that is manufactured at one level for distribution at another." Liberation theology, in contrast, "was not invented in the libraries of seminaries and then disseminated to the masses. It is not a 'trickle down' theology. These theologians spend hours with people who are engaged in difficult and dangerous political tasks" in their communities. This is the locus of praxis, the place where theological reflection and concrete action meet. Cornel West thus argues that liberation theology

> must be organically linked with prophetic churches and progressive movements. An uncommitted and detached liberation theologian is a contradiction in terms. Without some form of ecclesiastical and political praxis, critical consciousness becomes as sounding brass and theological reflection a tinkling cymbal.

The Self and Social Class

The liberation emphasis on praxis goes deeper than the question of involvement or noninvolvement. It also challenges the liberal-modern understanding of the human self. In liberation theology, the self is constituted not by any quality of rationality or subjective experience, but by a way of living in the world, including responsible action in community. The human subject is not the autonomous rational skeptic but the believing poor person, the person whose autonomy is limited by social and economic circumstances of oppression. This is a key to liberation theology's goal of overcoming oppression. As Chopp notes, "It is only by reconceiving the human subject through praxis that we may respond to suffering."

Liberation theology aligns itself with the poor and the oppressed and tends to see liberal theology as aligned with the privileged middle classes, and therefore as primarily addressing their needs. Rieger comments that "the struggle of oppressed people for liberation cannot easily be identified with the modern self's struggle for autonomy." Chopp nicely captures this contrast in her remark that from a liberation perspective, modern liberal theology "functions as an ideology for the bourgeois." And German theologian Dorothee Sölle makes the same point more starkly: "[Liberal] bourgeois theology is the work of the white middle class.... It takes no account of the impoverished masses of this earth; the starving appear at most as objects of charity."

On a deeper level, individualism itself is linked to social class. More than seventy years ago, H. Richard Niebuhr noted the link between denominationalism and social class in American religion. As Niebuhr saw it, middle-class churches tend to emphasize individual self-consciousness, personal salvation, and financial security, as well as an ethic of individual responsibility. At the same time, middle-class religion is associated with the social and economic establishment and as a result cannot engage problems of social justice at a deep level since overturning the existing system would be contrary to its own interests. Sharon Welch has commented on the class ideology that lies at the root of the "cultured despair of the middle class," an attitude that contributes to the abandonment of social justice work "when one is already the beneficiary of partial social change." Rieger claims that

> the modern self is quite unaware that it is part of a struggle
> for power at all. Having created a theological vision of har-
> mony and peace in the relation of God and humanity,...

liberal theology thus tunes out the contradictions and conflicts of real life, thereby reinforcing theologically the blind-
ness of the self for its own role in the power struggle of the
modern world.

Sociologist Robert Bellah makes a similar point by noting the
close link between religious individualism and economic privilege. His observations are worth quoting at length:

> Freedom of conscience and freedom of enterprise are more
> closely, even genealogically, linked than many of us would
> like to believe.... They are both expressions of an underlying
> ontological individualism. It is no accident...that the
> United States, with its high evaluation of the individual per-
> son, is nonetheless alone among North Atlantic societies in
> the percentage of our population who live in poverty and
> that we are dismantling what was already the weakest welfare
> state of any North Atlantic nation. Just when we are moving
> to an ever greater validation of the sacredness of the indi-
> vidual person, our capacity to imagine a social fabric that
> would hold individuals together is vanishing. And this is in
> no small part due to the fact that our religious individualism
> is linked to an economic individualism which...ultimately
> knows nothing of the sacredness of the individual.... What
> economic individualism destroys and what our kind of reli-
> gious individualism cannot restore, is solidarity, a sense of
> being members of the same body.

The way out, Bellah suggests, is to get past our erroneous idea that
we are isolated and self-sufficient individuals. "Ontological individualism is false both theologically and sociologically." It is a
"mistake" with "enormous cultural consequences."

The liberation perspective, in this sense, becomes an invitation for liberals to come to a more expansive understanding of
ourselves as human subjects. "The modern self," as Rieger puts it,
"needs to realize its basic connectedness to the other." This view
builds on and extends the principle of the social self discussed ear-

lier. Yet it is in line with the basic liberal understanding that all things are organically interdependent. It says that I am not a complete human being until I sense this connectedness and absorb it into my own self-understanding. My self is not just connected to the other, but *completed* in the other. As Frederick Herzog put it, "the commandment to love the other as oneself is...an invitation...to discover the other as co-constitutive of one's self."

This form of self-understanding tells us that we are called to account by the other who co-constitutes us. While in some sense this is a universal principle, from the liberation perspective we become accountable in the first instance to the poor and oppressed peoples of the world. This is different from the liberal-modern view, which made the autonomous subject accountable only to itself. Lyon explains, "While modernity aimed to release the subject from historical contingency, liberation theology aims to bring the subject to historical accountability." Yet because of our interdependence, we also deepen our own selves through this accountability to the other. This approach invites us to hold two paradoxical views, both contrary to the liberal-modern way of seeing the world, yet both necessary if we are to move forward in our justice work: We must learn to see the poor and oppressed other as a complete subject in her own right, and we must learn to see ourself in her and herself in us. Paradoxically, when we encounter each other in a subject-to-subject relationship, we also recognize that we are completed as selves through each other.

Liberation theology thus calls for "class conversion." It tells us liberals that if we really want to work for justice in the world, we need to rethink our own identity as human beings and move toward an intersubjective solidarity with the oppressed. A liberating praxis calls not just for social action but for a new way of being in the world, an engaged solidarity with the suffering and oppressed peoples of the world. The preferential option for the poor then becomes not simply an interpretive principle but a form of religious, pastoral, and political alignment.

In the final analysis, while liberation theology challenges us in important ways and offers useful critical insight, religious liberals must remember that we speak from a different tradition. While we can and should draw on the resources and insights of other traditions such as liberation theology, liberal theology must speak first to the tradition it serves, which is basically a middle-class religious tradition. We must ask: In what ways are we implicated in the social structures of oppression? What are our various privileges in the current social structures, and how are they connected with, even dependent on, the suffering of others? How might our own practices unwittingly perpetuate the oppressive structures we are seeking to overturn? How can we use our privilege to effect change and alleviate suffering? What are we willing to give up?

These are some of the questions we must ask if we want to liberate ourselves and reverse the inertia of the tension in theological liberalism that often interferes with our own best intentions to do truly liberating social justice work.

The Challenge of Racism

THE TENSIONS FACING LIBERAL THEOLOGY today are not simply abstractions. They affect the way we view the world, the way we relate to our religious communities, and the way we perceive and respond to what is happening around us in our culture. They also affect our ability to carry out our commitments to social justice. To sharpen the analysis of these challenges, we will focus on one critical issue: the efforts of religious liberals to confront and respond to the evil of white racism.

Cultural Adaptation and Race

The commitment to being involved in the culture and to making theology relevant to the contemporary situation is one of the hallmarks of liberalism. At the same time, religious liberals have tried to avoid becoming so absorbed into the larger culture that they lose the ability to step back from it and see its weak spots. We liberals may be involved in the culture, but we bring our religious values and moral convictions with us. This is the basis on which liberals seek to offer a prophetic critique of those aspects of the culture that fall short of these values.

The dilemma is that these two liberal tendencies, the accommodating and the prophetic, exist in tension with each other. Our history shows that the accommodating side has been the stronger of the two, and this has blunted the edge of our prophetic witness. This is not a new situation. A half century ago, H. Richard Niebuhr noted that the easy accommodation of religion and culture tends to produce a certain level of intellectual and social comfort. As a result, religious liberals tend to be nonrevolutionaries who support gradual reform or small-scale correctives rather than radical social change. Cornel West agrees, arguing that a strong prophetic voice in American religion can be recovered only by "counter[ing] and contest[ing] the widespread accommodation of American religion to the political and cultural status quo." And the problem lies deeper than simply weak justice work. West continues,

> This accommodation is suffocating much of the best in American religion; it promotes and encourages an existential emptiness and political irrelevance. This accommodation is, at bottom, idolatrous—it worships the gods created by American society and kneels before the altars erected by American culture.

The issue of race places the tension between adaptation and critique in stark relief, allowing us to see how deeply it is engrained in our theology and therefore in our ways of responding to the world.

A related tension that contributes to the liberal response to racial injustice is social class. Liberal religion has historically been largely a white middle-class movement, and this remains true today. Again, H. Richard Niebuhr noted the link between denominationalism and social class over seventy years ago. As he saw it, middle-class churches tend to emphasize individual self-consciousness, personal salvation, financial security, and an ethic of individual responsibility. Niebuhr's analysis of liberal theology in light of these class issues led him to the following conclusion:

> The cultural Christians tend to address themselves to the leading groups in a society; they speak to the cultured among

the despisers of religion; they use the language of the more sophisticated circles, of those who are acquainted with the science, the philosophy, and the political and economic movements of their time. They are missionaries to the aristocracy and the middle-class, or to the groups rising to power in a civilization.

The values of this middle-class tradition tend to tip the balance toward the accommodating and away from the prophetic. As sociologist Parker J. Palmer notes,

> The religion of the American middle class sometimes seems to mock the Gospels; it aims at enhancing the self-esteem of persons who have material comfort while ignoring conditions of poverty and pestilence which deprive a whole class of people of life itself, let alone feelings of self-worth.

In other words, middle-class religion's long association with the social and economic establishment has limited its ability to engage social justice issues at a deep level, because overturning the existing system would be contrary to its own interests. This danger remains present for European-American religious liberals as they seek to become antiracist today.

Another recurring tension in liberal theology is its ambiguity around spirituality, which profoundly affects the ability of religious liberals to sustain a commitment to antiracism work. It's true that religious liberals are concerned with finding the spiritual depth in their tradition, and some strands of liberal religious thought have been explicitly grounded in mysticism and spirituality from the beginning. Nevertheless, liberal theology in general has been more comfortable with analysis than with prayer, more grounded in the head than in the heart. Too many liberals fall into the trap of thinking that spirituality and rationality are somehow opposed to each other. But attending to the spiritual dimension of our religious lives is essential if our antiracism work is to be effective because the evil of racism lies deeper than institutional structures and systemic power relations. It has a spiritual dimension that liberals often fail to recognize. As a result, despite our clearest analysis and noblest intentions, we sometimes fail to truly engage and call out the evil that holds us in its grasp.

While these tensions may seem like insurmountable barriers, they reflect a telling and potentially liberating irony. Left unattended, they tend toward an equilibrium that sabotages our own best intentions and reinforces a comfortable status quo. Squarely confronting the continuing evil of white racism and our own complicity in it can shift the balance of these tensions and strengthen our prophetic witness in the world. It can also deepen and enliven our spiritual lives. Spiritual depth, theological analysis, and prophetic witness are interconnected, and all are deepened in the crucible of a shared day-to-day struggle for justice.

Liberal Theology's Ambivalent History

The impact of these tensions and ambiguities on liberal theology's response to racism in American society lies deeper than our current struggles. At several important points during the past two centuries, religious liberals were led by their own convictions into stances that made them less effective advocates for racial justice than they might have been. In some instances they were outright racist. Examining some of these earlier episodes may help us identify and avoid similar traps today.

EVOLUTION AND SOCIAL DARWINISM. Charles Darwin's book *Origin of Species*, describing the theory of natural selection, was published in 1859. Just over a decade later, in 1871, he published *The Descent of Man*, extending the general principles of his theory to the human species. These books had a profound impact on Christian religious thought. As historian Sidney Ahlstrom puts it, not since Newton "had the humanistic and religious traditions of the West been confronted by a greater need for adjustment and reformulation." While the response to Darwin was uneven, liberal theologians and religious leaders in general accepted his theory and sought to adapt their theologies to it. By 1885, for example, the radical Unitarian theologian Francis E. Abbot had published a book entitled *Scientific Theism*, fully incorporating Darwinian evolution into his understanding of God and the world. This ready acceptance of Darwin reflected the broader liberal characteristic of adapting theology to modern culture, including the scientific advances of the day.

Darwin's influence was felt far beyond the natural sciences. The religious thinkers of this period had to struggle not only with a theory of biological evolution but with a problematic adaptation of this theory known as *social Darwinism*, associated primarily with English philosopher Herbert Spencer. As Gary Dorrien describes it, Spencer "combined Darwinian natural selection with laissez-faire economic ideology" and other elements into a system that explained social structures and human cultural achievements in terms of the "survival of the fittest." This view had the practical effect of justifying the positions of those already in positions of power. Among other things, it led to a social philosophy that opposed state-supported assistance of any kind, including poverty relief and even education. More important, it justified the continued social exclusion and economic marginalization of most African-Americans, Native Americans, women of all races, and other disenfranchised groups such as Catholics, Mormons, Jews, and many recent immigrants.

In liberal religious circles, the struggle over social Darwinism was in many ways more significant than the struggle with biological evolution. While the social policies that emerged from this theory were contrary to the liberal religious impulse for justice and equality, many liberals supported it because of its apparent grounding in science. Thus, while many liberals were simultaneously "intimidated, attracted, and appalled" by social Darwinism, they nevertheless accepted it "as an authoritatively scientific description of the way the world works." Moreover, because it was linked to evolution, social Darwinism could be justified by an appeal to progress, another important liberal theme. One especially disturbing outgrowth of Spencer's theory was the doctrine of manifest destiny, which supported Anglo-Saxon America's self-understanding as the chosen people destined "to make all of humanity civilized and Christian."

Significantly, many of America's leading liberal church leaders and theologians endorsed manifest destiny because it seemed to promote social progress. Indeed, by linking this doctrine to the concept of God's providence, the advance of Anglo-Saxon cultural domination could be seen as God's will. It is here that we can see the latent—and in some cases explicit—racism of even the most liberal theologians of the time. The most prominent example was Congregational minister and social gospel leader Josiah Strong, who was a leading figure in revitalizing an interdenominational Protestant focus on the social issues confronting American cities. His 1885 book *Our Country: Its Possible Future and Its Present Crisis* has been called "the most influential social gospel book of the nineteenth century." Strong also believed in Anglo-Saxon America's manifest destiny to lead the world into "a new stage of its history." Framing what he saw as "the final competition of races" in terms of the Spencerian notion of the survival of the fittest, Strong proclaimed,

> Is it not reasonable to believe that this race is destined to dispossess many weaker ones, assimilate others, and mould the remainder, until in a very true and important sense, it has Anglo-Saxonized mankind?

Strong and other leading liberal religious figures were products of their own cultures, and as a result they inevitably "accepted and purveyed the Anglo-Saxon cultural racism that pervaded nineteenth-century American society." Social Darwinism compounded the problem because its scientific cast gave it a sheen of respectability. The result was an insidious form of racism couched in the liberal values of scientific advancement and social progress.

THE CIVIL RIGHTS MOVEMENT. Liberal theology's ambivalence around issues of race persisted into the twentieth century. Like their social gospel predecessors, the liberals of the post–World War I era defended racial equality and worked at improving race relations in the larger society. But on the whole, they could escape neither their own cultures nor the contradictions of their own theology:

> White liberal theologians were so deeply defined by these liberal values of intellectual freedom, individual rights equality, and peace that it was difficult... to absorb that the typical liberal response to racial injustice was superficial and often patronizing.

A prominent example of this ambivalence is the liberal Baptist preacher-theologian Harry Emerson Fosdick. In 1931 Fosdick became the first minister to occupy what was to become one of America's most influential pulpits, that of New York City's Riverside Church. Condemnations of racial discrimination were heard regularly in his sermons, yet his own racism was also evident. As Dorrien notes, he "sprinkled his sermons and conversation with 'funny' stories that were either attributed to 'colored folks' or which implicitly made them the butt of his so-called humor." He also believed in the inherent superiority of the Anglo-Saxon race, continuing this unfortunate legacy of nineteenth-century thought. The result of this ambivalence was that "on the whole Fosdick's ministry aided the causes of desegregation and racial progress, but not nearly as much as it could have, and always with a whiff of white supremacy." This tension also reflected the larger liberal response to race during this period. As Dorrien notes, during the 1940s and 1950s,

> Liberal theologians and church leaders...became fairly good at making formal statements against racial discrimination. But they were pitifully ineffective at challenging the racism of everyday America. On the whole, the theological leaders of American liberal Christianity gave low priority to

the battle against racism. They rarely treated the issue with the kind of passion they devoted to peace or intellectual freedom, and their own rhetoric was often casually racist.

This problem persisted, affecting and eventually weakening liberal religious participation in the civil rights movement. In general, liberal theologians during the mid-twentieth century "thought of themselves as stubborn idealists who held out for the common good and the ideals of modern Christianity." But this vision had its blind spots:

> This self-conception compounded their difficulty in perceiving their complicity in America's sins. Liberal Protestantism preached that racism is evil, but its resistance to the evil of American segregation was pitifully tepid, as Martin Luther King Jr. frequently observed.

Part of the reason for this ineffectiveness around race was that these mid-twentieth-century liberals, like their nineteenth-century predecessors, were caught up in the tensions and ambivalence within liberal theology itself.

A telling illustration of these tendencies is the collapse during the 1960s of the liberal-progressive coalition that had emerged around the civil rights movement following the end of World War II. As legal scholar Anthony Cook sees it, the coalition disintegrated because it couldn't fully deal with the legacy of racism in America. Ironically, this disintegration began at the very moment of one of the movement's greatest victories, the passage of the 1965 Voting Rights Act.

While this law was a victory, it was only a formal victory. As Martin Luther King Jr. and others understood, a "color-blind" federal law prohibiting discrimination wouldn't really change much unless poverty and class were also addressed. Yet white liberals were largely unwilling to do this. They were afraid of King's new call for a radically inclusive coalition; they were even more afraid of the explicitly race-conscious agenda of the black power move-

ment. As Cook puts it, "The liberal coalition reached its philosophical limits with the signing of the 1965 Voting Rights Act."
Theologian James Cone's trenchant analysis of these events is similar. White resistance was so great that King "had to move closer to
Malcolm [X]'s perspective and begin to see white liberals as phony
advocates of freedom for the black poor."

Current Issues

These failures reflect the historic liberal tensions and ambiguities
around cultural accommodation and social class. They also point
to some deeper issues that continue to affect us today.

WHITE SILENCE. As the social agenda moved during the 1960s
and 1970s from the issues of formal equality and basic human de-
cency to the more concrete matters of genuine equality and systemic oppression, many white theologians and religious liberals
became reluctant to talk about race at all. This silence remains all
too common today. James Cone states the matter bluntly:

> Though racism inflicts massive suffering, few American the-
> ologians have even bothered to address white supremacy as
> a moral evil and as a radical contradiction to our humanity
> and religious identities.... Why do white ministers and the-
> ologians ignore racism?... Shouldn't they be the first to at-
> tack this evil?

Liberal theologians and religious leaders may hesitate to talk
about existing disparities among racial and ethnic groups because to do so feels somehow like buying into racial stereotypes.
The continuing gaps in income and education between European
Americans and African Americans or Latinos/Latinas, for example, might conjure uncomfortable echoes of expressions of
Anglo-Saxon superiority a century ago. Or perhaps these disparities remind us of the continuing structural racism we once
thought, or at least hoped, had been addressed. From the per-

spective of the "color-blind" ideals of an earlier era, this kind of race talk can seem distinctly "unliberal."

Cone argues that the problem of white guilt, especially when combined with the difficult issue of accountability, contributes to a reluctance among liberal theologians and ministers to speak and write about racism. We are all familiar with the terrible legacy of slavery, segregation, genocide of Native peoples, and other forms of racial oppression that blot the American historical and social landscape, and we know the deep social and economic inequalities it has left in its wake. Yet it can be emotionally difficult to connect this legacy to ourselves in the present. Cone continues,

> Whites do not like to think of themselves as evil people or to believe that their place in the world is due to the colonization of Indians, the enslavement of blacks, and the exploitation of people of color here and around the world. Whites like to think of themselves as honorable, decent, and fair-minded people. They resent being labeled racists.

One way to avoid confronting the issue of indirect accountability—the present residual benefit from previous unjust practices—is to avoid talking about it. Cone suggests that whites often avoid talk of racial justice because it implies a radical redistribution of wealth and power. "Progressive whites do not mind talking as long as it doesn't cost much, as long as the structures of power remain intact."

White religious liberals may also avoid talking about race because they don't want to confront black rage. Cone notes that whites "do not mind talking as long as blacks don't get too emotional, too carried away with their stories of hurt." But these are stories we must learn to hear if we are to recover our own voices. As Cone says, "Black anger upsets only whites who choose not to identify with black suffering." But white liberals tend to be more comfortable in conversations that are more intellectual than emotional, conversations that reflect a tone of decorum and restraint. Cone claims this was the reason white religious leaders "preferred

Martin King to Malcolm X. Malcolm spoke with too much rage for their social taste."

In the face of this silence, Cone makes the following plea:

> I urge white theologians, ministers, and other morally concerned persons to break their silence immediately and continuously.... The development of a hard-hitting antiracist theology on the part of white scholars of religion is long overdue.

Fortunately, many theologians and ministers are again speaking out, and there are signs of a renewed dedication to racial justice in the white liberal churches. Cone cites events such as the three-day Unitarian Universalist consultation on theology and antiracism in 2001, in which he participated, as one promising sign. Another is the increasing racial and ethnic diversity seen in some liberal seminaries, including Union Theological Seminary in New York City and Iliff School of Theology in Denver. And many churches and denominational bodies are engaged in ongoing education and self-examination around racism. But we have a long way to go.

SPIRITUALITY. Liberal theology's inherent tensions and ambiguities will continue to weaken the liberal prophetic voice and interfere with our antiracism work unless we recognize that racism poisons our hearts as well as our institutions. In other words, we must attend to racism's spiritual dimensions. To do this, we must see racism not only as a matter of institutional structures and social power disparities, but as a profound evil.

This is a difficult message for liberals to hear. It is not simply about making a moral judgment that racism is wrong nor about making an anthropological claim that human beings have the capacity to do horrible things and create oppressive institutions. These statements are true of course; in fact, they represent the way religious liberals usually think about systemic evils. Instead, this is a theological claim: Racism is a profound structural evil embedded deeply within our culture and within ourselves. It is a "power" in the biblical sense, an impersonal spiritual force that separates us from the good we seek.

It is hard for liberals to talk in these terms because we have no real theology of evil and therefore no language or conceptual reference points adequate to the task. But any other approach is inadequate. Treating racism as an evil, a power that has us in its grasp, may help us realize more clearly what we are up against. This does not mean that we need to think of it as a disembodied supernatural demon or the like. White racism is of course a cultural construct, the invention of human beings in specific historical settings and social contexts. But to approach it as a human construct and nothing more misses its profound power over us. We are tempted to think it can be dismantled with the right motivation, proper analysis, and good programs. It will take all of these and more; but by themselves, they are not enough.

Racism, once unleashed onto the world and embedded within human structures and institutions, takes on a life of its own. Like all cultural and institutional structures, it eventually becomes self-perpetuating. Despite our best and most persistent efforts to dismantle it, racism keeps coming back in newer and more subtle forms. As urban theologian Bill Wylie-Kellermann says, "No force in U.S. history has proven more relentless or devastatingly resilient than white racism. It is empirically a demon that again and again rises up transmogrified in ever more predatory and beguiling forms, truly tempting our despair."

When we begin to see it from this perspective, we can recognize that the evil of racism gets inside us despite our best efforts to block it out, eating away at our hearts, eroding our capacity for expanded community. New Testament scholar Walter Wink even suggests that the hold this sort of evil has on us amounts to a kind of possession:

> Our involvement with evil goes far beyond our conscious, volitional participation in evil. To a much greater extent than

we are aware, we are possessed by the values and powers of our unjust order. It is not enough then simply to repent of the ways we have consciously chosen to collude with evil; we must be freed from our unconscious enthrallment as well.

When we acknowledge this unconscious captivity, we begin to open space for healing and then for expanded community based on love. The metaphor of powers can help us understand that the evil of racism is not only structural and institutional, it is also spiritual. All of our analysis, no matter how sophisticated, and all of our programs, no matter how well designed, will never be sufficient to make us antiracist. We must also be "willing to do the difficult soul work necessary for spiritual transformation."

This aspect of our task reveals still another ambivalence for religious liberals. As much as we say we want more spirituality in our lives, we are often reluctant to go too deep to find it. Part of this may be due to our traditional emphasis on rationality, which many of us erroneously place in opposition to spirituality. Another factor may be an implicit awareness that sustained spiritual practice can take us deep inside, exposing aspects of ourselves we may rather not see. But racism cannot be overcome without this work. As Wink says,

> Any attempt to transform a social system without addressing both its spirituality and its outer forms is doomed to failure.
> ... Only by confronting the spirituality of an institution *and* its concretions can the total entity be transformed, and that requires a kind of spiritual discernment and praxis that the materialistic ethos in which we live knows nothing about.

We must recognize the dimensions of the struggle we are engaged in. We have been shaped by the very powers and structures we now want to dismantle. It is important to remember that there is no biological or genetic basis for the racial categories we use. Not only racism, but the category of race itself is a culturally constructed concept. Those of us who grew up in America were unwittingly "cultured" into the racial identities we now carry. The fragmentation of our society produces a parallel fragmentation within our individual selves. Those of us who were cultured into whiteness were educated into an alienated state of mind, a fragmented way of being in the world. The same is true of those cultured into other racial identities. In a fractured society, we all become fractured selves. This is why the social transformation we seek requires spiritual transformation as well. Without this, our antiracism work becomes difficult to sustain or retreats into the safety of disengaged analysis or internal debate.

COMMUNITY. Our efforts to become genuinely antiracist are hampered by a liberal ambivalence around the issue of community. One of the factors at work here is the human tendency to want community on our own terms, a community of people "like us." But for liberals, additional difficulties emerge out of the tensions inherent in our tradition. Liberals want to create a strong and inclusive community, but we often want to do it without giving up anything, without letting down the barriers we erect around ourselves in the name of individual autonomy. We wade into the waters of community up to our knees, but we're afraid to let go of the dock and plunge in with our whole bodies. Cook puts it in stark terms:

> The central problem of liberalism . . . is that the liberal conception of community is based too much on fear and too little on love. It is fear of the 'other' that generates in liberal thought the fundamental paradox of liberal theory. The liberal subject both desires and fears, needs and is threatened by community.

Yet the problem lies deeper. Our deep-seated fear of community, when combined with our tendency toward formalism and abstraction, leads to a fear of otherness that we have barely begun to recognize and address. Fear of the Other manifests itself in such liberal ideals as autonomy, self-reliance, and the like, and prevents us from seeing that we are truly social selves. Liberal political and social theory, too often echoed in liberal religion, tends to protect the individual *from* the community, from true engagement with the Other. This kind of negative freedom tends to produce a constricted sense of self. But a love-based understanding of community would extend the individual and expand the self outward *toward* the Other.

Another important factor is the traditional liberal emphasis on rationality. This is one of liberal theology's great strengths. It leads liberals to do good conceptual analysis, and this is important work. Careful analysis helps clarify the issues at stake, which is essential if we are to address the systemic and structural dimensions of racism. But as the liberal confusion following the Voting Rights Act shows, this sort of analysis can get stuck in a formal rationality that can easily keep us at a respectable and safe distance from the problems we are addressing. Like Linus, who in a famous *Peanuts* cartoon remarks, "I love mankind—it's people I can't stand," we liberals are often better at formality and abstraction than at getting our hands dirty and our feet moving. We sincerely want things to be right in the world, but we also want them to be tidy. Both justice work and community are often messy, and our discomfort with messiness weakens the prophetic power of our words and actions.

What sort of community is possible in our postmodern situation, with its radically individualistic consumerism and increasingly fragmented society? It is telling that contemporary countermodern and postmodern theologies—both of which are conceived as alternatives to liberal-modern theology—place religious community at the core of their programs. So-called postliberal theology, for example, harking back to certain premodern approaches, understands religion in terms of particular historical communities and traditions. The community is primary, and individual identity is formed in relation to it. This approach entails a risk of creating a circle-the-wagons, inward-facing community that seeks to protect itself from the outside world. This posture would not be appropriate in any liberal vision of religious community, but it does challenge religious liberals to rethink their traditional emphasis on the individual. Community also plays a vital role in postmodern liberation theologies. Small groups of people, meeting in "base communities," constitute the core practice out of which both social action and theological reflection emerge. It seems that religious liberals, grounded in the modern view of the autonomous subject, have been the holdouts, slow to let go of their individualistic approach to religious life. But this is changing. Contemporary liberal theologians widely recognize the social nature of the self. The emergence of various forms of small-group ministries in the liberal churches is an indication that this social-communal perspective is not limited to the theologians. These are very promising signs.

Sharon Welch offers some useful reflections on both the power and the dangers of community. She is struggling with the question of how we can maintain a sense of connectedness in a fragmented society and ways in which just and democratic social relationships can be structured. She writes,

> The roles of the ritual community and of the spiritual leader are not to measure the moral worth of an individual or a community, but to help the individual and the community see what is going on, what the relationships of power are, and, from that seeing, find ways of balancing relationships and ways of balancing power.

At the same time, members of the community must be willing to "be critical of key aspects of that community's values, practices, and history" when necessary.

A bigger question is, What happens to a community when its members have different or even incompatible views of community? Is internal diversity a strength or a threat? As Welch says, "How much difference can a community hold? How much critique?" Welch comes down on the side of pluralism and rejects the "common ground" basis of community:

What bothers me about the calls for common ground is that this very concept of community is predicated on denying what I see as the richness of community, a richness created as much by difference and surprise as by similarity and affirmation.

The emphasis on commonalities and common ground presumes a truncated vision of human relationships. The connections that give life meaning ... at times take the form of the shock of recognition. But just as often, the connections that give life meaning come from the shock of difference.

This is clearly a challenge to the kinds of religious identity-forming communities advocated by the postliberals. It also affirms, without saying so, the wide theological diversity typical of many liberal churches today. Yet Welch recognizes the need for at least some minimal common ground: "This is not to say that similarity is not comforting and is not essential. It is. What I am saying is that it is the blend of similarity and difference that enriches life."

Welch speaks of "communities of resistance and solidarity." The proper response to what she calls the "spiritual malaise of racism" lies in "participation in a community of practice in which political work against white supremacy is sustained by acts of worship that feed the soul." This sort of participation can also help address the problem of class isolation. As Welch puts it,

A genuine conversation between those who are privileged by way of class, gender, or race and those who have experienced oppression or discrimination on the basis of those characteristics is possible when the privileged work to end the oppression or discrimination they denounce. As we do more than vote for those opposed to racism, challenging racism directly in our workplaces, in our families, and in our own lives, we can be trusted in a way that enables those oppressed because of race to speak with us more honestly. In our work we see more clearly the costs of racism and the intransigence of structures of oppression.

Paul Lakeland also offers useful observations about religious community in the postmodern situation. For Lakeland, "postmodernity challenges almost every element of [the traditional understanding] of the role of the faith community." In particular, the traditional role of the church as the locus of moral authority is disappearing, except, perhaps, among certain fundamentalist groups. So what is left? Lakeland suggests that the most successful engagements with the postmodern world have taken place through groups that have adopted some model of what Lakeland calls "faithful sociality." This term is meant to highlight two important dimensions of the religious life. "'Sociality' stresses the inevitably social and political presence of the members to one another and within the larger society. But the qualifier 'faithful' reminds us that spirituality is as important as political praxis." Lakeland holds up the various forms of liberation ecclesiality and the practices of the African-American church as representative. Unfortunately, he does not discuss the various forms of religious community practiced by groups such as Quakers and Mennonites, who might offer another model of "faithful sociality."

My own experience of Quaker community at Pendle Hill reflects this. During my five years there, I found myself moving away from my old go-it-alone path—once so comfortable—to a felt need for and celebration of the gifts of community. Pendle Hill is not a church; it is a broad-based religious and educational residential community. Staff, students, and guests share practices of daily worship, ongoing study and service, and the daily work of the household in such a way that the community comes to inform all aspects of our lives. It is also a broadly diverse community, encompassing a variety of faith orientations and demographic factors such as age, race, sexual orientation, ethnicity, and nationality. Only about half are Quaker. Further, not everyone agrees on the details of what the community should be, but somehow this community has been transformative for many who have come to it. This is partly a product of an explicit intention to be this kind of community. It also involves a lot of hard work.

For Welch, the kinds of social responses that emerge out of these sorts of communities involve taking the long view. Responsible social action means not trying to solve everything at once. This is an impossible goal, and it can lead us to think we know the right ultimate outcome. Instead, responsible action involves creating the conditions for continued struggle and the possibility of further change in the future. And this work "is sustained and enabled by participation in an extensive community." While "we cannot guarantee an end to racism . . . we can prevent our own capitulation to structured evil."

Here is a basis for hope. Our antiracism work, if it is spiritually grounded and sustained through community, can help create a significant counterforce to the accommodationist inertia that often weakens our liberal prophetic voice. Indeed, Anthony Cook argues that the progressive religious voice cannot be truly recovered without attending to the unfinished business of racial justice. But we will have to dedicate our heads, hands, and hearts to the task. It means, too, that we will need to find ways to build and nurture communities that can sustain us. At their best, our communities—including our religious communities—can nurture our identities and help overcome isolation. They can also help define and encourage groundedness and even provide a basis for engagement in the world.

Final Thoughts

LIBERAL THEOLOGY IS NOT for the faint of heart. It points us in a general direction without telling us the specific destination. It refuses to make our commitments for us but holds us accountable for the commitments we make. The liberal religious tradition is an invitation, not a mandate. It invites us to live with ambiguity without giving in to facile compromise; to engage in dialogue without trying to control the conversation; to be open to change without accepting change too casually; to take commitment seriously but not blindly; and to be engaged in the culture without succumbing to the culture's values. Liberal religion calls us to strength without rigidity, conviction without ideology, openness without laziness. It asks us to pay attention. It is an eyes-wide-open faith, a faith without certainty.

This book has been both descriptive and critical. At the descriptive level, I have sought to provide a basic introduction to liberal theology. I have done this not simply by describing liberal theology's identifying characteristics, but also by locating it within its historical, intellectual, and social context. Liberal theology—like any other theology—is not merely a collection of free-standing ideas. It exists in specific places and times, and it belongs to an ongoing and multi-faceted religious tradition.

A vital feature of the liberal theological tradition is constructive self-examination. This is an important process. It helps keep
liberal theology relevant to the needs of each succeeding generation. It guards against staleness and rigidity. It becomes a method
of built-in accountability. In this spirit, then, I have addressed a
few of liberalism's internal weaknesses and contradictions, and at
some points have been quite critical. I have also tackled head-on
the difficult issues of race and class that continue to confront liberal theology and sometimes cause us to stumble over our own
best intentions. In each case I have offered some constructive sug-
gestions as well. At the same time, I have tried to bring liberal theology into conversation with other currents in the contemporary
theological stream. Some of these, such as liberation theology and
postliberal theology, are highly critical of liberalism. My working
assumption has been that while liberal theology need not adjust to
all its critics' complaints—it could not remain liberal if it did—
there is nevertheless much we can learn from them.

Critical self-examination also points to liberal theology's
great strengths. These include its principled open-mindedness, its
intellectual honesty, and its commitment to social justice. These
are among the hallmarks of the liberal tradition, and they are
worth preserving. Today's theological landscape is highly plural-
istic. Many voices struggle to be heard. Some seek dialogue and
engagement; others seek merely to shout the loudest. It is precisely in these circumstances that liberal theology's prophetic and
mediating voice is most needed. The early twenty-first century in
the United States is a time of increasing dogmatic rigidity in both
politics and religion. We are confronted by a worldview of simplistic dualisms. Dissent—even asking hard questions—is seen as
a threat; data that do not support pre-set ideas are ignored;
deeper analysis of complex issues is avoided. Liberal theology
rejects this way of being. It seeks deeper and more nuanced
explanations. It understands the inherent complexity and
interrelatedness of things. It has learned to live with tensions and
ambiguities. Liberal theology's willingness to engage in ongoing

and thoughtful critique offers an important corrective voice in the public dialogue.

This is important work. But none of us can do this work alone. As much as we need constructive self-examination and critical dialogue, we need each other. We may never come to think alike or to act alike. I hope not. But by participating in each other's faith journeys, by reaching out to each other and sharing in each other's struggles to name and claim our theologies, we can strengthen our public prophetic voice and deepen our sense of community and our commitment to a shared faith tradition.

May it be so.

Notes

Introduction

p.xi ...*simply open at both ends.* James Luther Adams, *On Being Human Religiously*, ed. Max Stackhouse (Boston: Beacon Press, 1976), 11.

p.xii ...*the "progressive element" in religious liberalism.* Stackhouse, 5.

p.xiii ...*creatures who cannot live without meaning.* James Fowler, *Stages of Faith* (San Francisco: HarperCollins, 1981), 292.

p.xiii ...*can be given meaningful form.* Clifford Geertz, *The Interpretation of Cultures* (New York: Basic Books, 1973), 123.

p.xiii ...*the meaning of human existence.* Gordon D. Kaufman, *In Face of Mystery: A Constructive Theology* (Cambridge, MA: Harvard University Press, 1993), 225.

p.xiii ...*the aim of existence.* Paul Tillich, *Systematic Theology*, vol. 1 (Chicago: University of Chicago Press, 1951), 14.

p.xiii ...*to be the primal truth.* William James, *The Varieties of Religious Experience* [1902] (New York: Penguin Books, 1982), 34-35.

p.xiii ...*the essential pattern of human life.* Susanne K. Langer, *Philosophy in a New Key*, 2nd ed. (New York: Mentor Books, 1951), 136.

p.xiv ...*what is supreme in worth.* Richard R. Niebuhr, "The Tragic Play of Symbols," *Harvard Theological Review*, vol. 75 (Jan. 1982), 28.

p.xiv ...*a sense of purposefulness and value.* Kaufman, 432.

p.xvi ... *centers of value.* H. Richard Niebuhr, *Radical Monotheism and Western Culture* (New York: Harper and Row, 1970), 100-13.

p.xviii ... *careful criticism and systematic reconstruction.* Kaufman, 123.

p.xix ... *issues facing twenty-first-century Christians.* Sallie McFague, *Life Abundant: Rethinking Theology and Economy for a Planet in Peril* (Minneapolis: Fortress Press, 2001), 15.

p.xx ... *pressing issues of our day.* McFague, 39.

p.xx ... *theology... cannot be noncommittal.* Harvey Cox, *Religion in the Secular City: Toward a Postmodern Theology* (New York: Simon and Schuster, 1984), 21.

p.xx ... *thinking, doing, and praying belong together.* McFague, 25.

The Religious Mind-set

p.1 ... *scientific, historical, philosophical, and religious truth.* David Tracy, *Blessed Rage for Order* (San Francisco: Harper and Row, 1988), 25-26.

p.2 ... *a spirit, an attitude, a state of mind.* Rufus M. Jones, *Re-thinking Religious Liberalism* (Boston: Beacon Press, 1935), 6.

p.2 ... *to break new paths.* James Luther Adams, *The Prophethood of All Believers*, ed. George Beach (Boston: Beacon Press, 1986), 72.

p.3 ... *historical overview of liberal theology.* For a more thorough treatment, I recommend Gary Dorrien's remarkable historical study of liberal theology, the first two volumes of a projected trilogy. *The Making of American Liberal Theology: Imagining Progressive Religion, 1805-1900,* vol. 1, and *The Making of American Liberal Theology: Idealism, Realism, and Modernity, 1900-1950,* vol. 2 (Louisville, KY: Westminster John Knox Press, 2001 and 2003).

p.4 ... *alternative to orthodox Calvinism.* Dorrien, vol. 1, 1.

p.4 ... Friedrich Schleiermacher, *On Religion: Speeches to Its Cultured Despisers* [1799], trans. Richard Crouter (New York: Cambridge University Press, 1988).

p.4 ... *nontheological claims to truth.* Claude Welch, *Protestant Thought in the Nineteenth Century*, vol. 1 (New Haven, CT: Yale University Press, 1972), 62.

p.5 ... *testing ground for liberal religious ideas.* William R. Hutchison, *The Modern Impulse in American Protestantism* (Cambridge, MA: Harvard University Press, 1972), 3.

p.5 ... *unrivaled spiritual leader.* Dorrien, vol. 1, 39.

p.5 ... *its academic German counterpart.* Dorrien, vol. 1, xxii.

p.6 ... *only one of the major Social Gospel theologians was Unitarian, Harvard's Francis Greenwood Peabody.* From a denominational perspective, there were also no Universalist theologians in that movement. A case can be made, however, for Clarence Skinner (1881-1949), dean of Crane Theological School at Tufts University. His leadership helped move Universalism from simply a theological doctrine to a concept of a progressive social order.

p.7 ... *social ambitions of mainstream American Protestantism.* Dorrien, vol. 2, 1.

p.7 ... *the "golden age" of American liberal theology.* Sydney E. Ahlstrom, *A Religious History of the American People* (New Haven, CT: Yale University Press, 1972), 763.

p.7 ... *success set them up for a hard fall.* Dorrien, vol. 2, 2.

p.8 ... *post-Christian and interreligious perspectives.* Dorrien, vol. 1, xx.

p.8 ... *theological reflection since the Reformation.* Dorrien, vol. 1, xv.

p.9 ... *the importance of Christian missions.* Dorrien, vol. 2, 10-11.

p.10 ... *value for the liberal religious movement.* For a fuller discussion of these issues, see Dorrien, vol. 2, 10-20, 531-534.

p.11 ... *in the least way resemble religion.* Schleiermacher, 77.

p.11 ... *thinking of that which created you.* Schleiermacher, 77-78.

p.12 ... *accorded with its image of Christ.* Dorrien, vol. 1, 399.

p.12 ... *religious thought to a secular world.* Paul Lakeland, *Postmodernity: Christian Identity in a Fragmented Age* (Minneapolis: Fortress Press, 1997), 40.

p.13 ... *seen to be incredible.* Sallie McFague, *The Body of God: An Ecological Theology* (Minneapolis: Fortress Press, 1993), 76.

p.13 ... *among the liberals to equate those realms.* David Robinson, *The Unitarians and the Universalists* (Westport, CT: Greenwood Press, 1985), 27. For a brief but helpful discussion of the Athenaeum, see Susan Wilson, *Boston Sites and Insights* (Boston: Beacon Press, 1994), 151-155.

p.14 ... *in complete consonance with Darwinian evolution.* Ahlstrom, 765.

p.15 ... *now at work in humanity.* Walter Rauschenbusch, *A Theology for the Social Gospel* [1917] (Nashville: Abington Press, 1945), 165.

p.15 … *their freest and highest development.* Rauschenbusch, 142.

p.15 … *to critique unhealthy economic structures.* Sallie McFague, *Life Abundant*, parts II and III; M. Douglas Meeks, *God the Economist: The Doctrine of God and Political Economy* (Minneapolis: Fortress Press, 1989).

p.16 … *some form of final unity.* See M. H. Abrams, *Natural Supernaturalism: Tradition and Revolution in Romantic Literature* (New York: W. W. Norton, 1971).

p.17 … *the world as holistic and organic.* See Franklin L. Baumer, *Modern European Thought: Continuity and Change in Ideas, 1600-1950* (New York: Macmillan, 1977), chapter 2.

p.19 … *some thirty years later.* See Ian G. Barbour, *Religion and Science: Historical and Contemporary Issues* (New York: HarperCollins, 1997), chapter 3.

p.20 … *no place where God is not.* McFague, *Life Abundant*, 149. This is also a recurring biblical theme, seen most famously, perhaps, in Psalm 139.

p.20 … *the total movement of our lives.* Marjorie Hewitt Suchocki, *In God's Presence: Theological Reflections on Prayer* (St. Louis: Chalice Press, 1996), 25.

p.21 …*toward its greater good.* Suchocki, 27.

p.21 … *within which we come to dwell.* Gordon D. Kaufman, *In Face of Mystery: A Constructive Theology,* (Cambridge, MA: Harvard University Press, 1993), 57.

p.21 … *nothing is exempt from criticism.* James Luther Adams, *On Being Human Religiously*, ed. Max Stackhouse (Boston: Beacon Press, 1976), 12.

p.21 … *seen through the same light.* Marjorie Hewitt Suchocki, *God-Christ-Church: A Practical Guide to Process Theology* (New York: Crossroad Press, 1982), 50.

p.22 … *within their own movement.* See Stephen A. Marini, *Radical Sects of Revolutionary New England* (Cambridge, MA: Harvard University Press, 1982), part 2.

p.22 … *the right of private judgment.* See Conrad Wright, *The Liberal Christians: Essays on American Unitarian History* (Boston: Unitarian Universalist Association, 1970), chapter 1.

p.23 … *all the claims they advance.* Kaufman, 28.

p.23 … *without which religion… cannot be liberal.* Adams, *On Being Human*, 14.

p.24 ... *a certain given, fateful character.* James Luther Adams, *The Prophethood of All Believers*, ed. George Beach (Boston: Beacon Press, 1986), 48.

p.24 ... *to make decisions and take actions.* Kaufman, 175.

p.26 ... *perfection of the Supreme Being.* William Ellery Channing, "Likeness to God," in *William Ellery Channing: Selected Writings*, ed. David Robinson (Mahwah, NJ: Paulist Press, 1985), 145-65, 151.

p.26 ... *a tender and impartial charity.* William Ellery Channing, "Unitarian Christianity," in ibid., 70-102.

p.27 ... *springs from their exertion.* Channing, "Unitarian Christianity," 94.

p.27 ... *the liberal tradition ever since.* See Dieter T. Hessel, *Theological Education for Social Ministry*, rev. ed. (Louisville, KY: Westminster John Knox, 1992).

p.28 ... *the progressive transformation of society.* Dorrien, vol. 1, 407.

p.28 ... *advocating any radical social change.* See Henry May, *Protestant Churches and Industrial America* (New York: Harper and Row, 1967).

p.29 ... *in terms of its theological bases.* James Luther Adams, "Theological Bases of Social Action," reprinted in Adams, *On Being Human*, 100-116.

p.29 ... *the institutionalizing of gradual revolution.* From an address entitled "The Indispensable Discipline of Social Responsibility: Voluntary Associations," delivered in 1962, in Adams, *Prophethood*, 258.

p.30 ... *the ultimate ordering power of the universe.* James Gustafson, *Ethics from a Theocentric Perspective*, 2 vols. (Chicago: University of Chicago Press, 1981-1984), from vol. 2, 1.

p.30 ... *and guidance for our lives.* Sharon D. Welch, *A Feminist Ethic of Risk* (Minneapolis: Fortress Press, 1990), 176.

p.30 ... *the "long struggle for justice" in any case.* Welch, 20.

p.30 ... *think of herself as a theologian.* See Sharon D. Welch, *Sweet Dreams in America: Making Ethics and Spirituality Work* (New York: Routledge Press, 1999).

Sources of Liberal Theology in the Modern Period

p.31 ... *relationships among measurable variables.* Ian Barbour, *Religion and Science: Historical and Contemporary Issues* (New York: HarperCollins, 1997), 10.

p.32 ...*in which he was interested.* Barbour, 11.

p.33 ...*apart from earlier historical periods.* Jürgen Habermas, *The Philosophical Discourse of Modernity* (Cambridge, MA: The MIT Press, 1987), chapter 1.

p.33 ...*moral guidance from within.* David West, *An Introduction to Continental Philosophy* (Cambridge, UK: Polity Press, 1996), 16.

p.34 ...*relying upon his own insight.* Habermas, 17.

p.35 ...*a civilization of authority.* Ernst Troeltsch, *Protestantism and Progress: The Significance of Protestantism for the Rise of the Modern World* [1912] (Philadelphia: Fortress Press, 1986), 22 (italics in original).

p.35 ...*courage to use your own reason.* Immanuel Kant, "What Is Enlightenment?" [1784] in *On History*, ed. Lewis White Beck (New York: Macmillan, 1963), 3.

p.36 ...*the cognitive-instrumental dimension.* Habermas, 314.

p.37 ...*self-confident optimism and belief in progress.* Troeltsch, 26.

p.37 ...*when guided by reason.* Cornel West, *The Cornel West Reader* (New York: Basic Civitas Books, 1999), 58.

p.37 ...*to unknown heights.* Troeltsch, 27.

p.37 ...*the power of human reason to produce freedom.* David Lyon, *Postmodernity*, 2nd ed. (Minneapolis: University of Minnesota Press, 1999), 25.

p.37 ...*onward and upward forever.* James Freeman Clarke, *Vexed Questions in Theology* (Boston: George H. Ellis, 1886), 16.

p.38 ...*one of modernity's most troubling legacies.* The racial implications of this idea will be examined in the "Liberation Theology" section.

p.38 ...*religion as a...universal phenomenon.* For more discussion of these issues, see Peter Byrne, *Natural Religion and the Nature of Religion: The Legacy of Deism* (New York: Routledge Press, 1989).

p.40 ...*terms that are independent of context.* See Stephen Toulmin, *Cosmopolis: The Hidden Agenda of Modernity* (New York: The Free Press, 1990).

p.40 ...*to criticism everything must submit.* Immanuel Kant, *Critique of Pure Reason* [1787], trans. Norman Kemp Smith (New York: St. Martin's Press, 1965), 9.

p.40 ...*partial truths of its own dogma.* Charlene Spretnak, *The Resurgence of the Real: Body, Nature, and Place in a Hypermodern World* (Reading, MA: Addison-Wesley, 1997), 43.

p.40 ... *built into modern thought.* Lyon, 8.

p.42 ... *the most conspicuous motor driving.* Lyon, 28.

p.42 ... *and favorable sales opportunities.* Ernst Troeltsch, "The Essence of the Modern Spirit" [1907], in Ernst Troeltsch, *Religion in History*, trans. J. L. Adams (Minneapolis: Fortress Press, 1991): 237-272.

p.43 ... *accelerating rates of economic growth.* D. West, 9.

p.43 ... *a colossal practical materialism.* Troeltsch, "Essence of Modern Spirit," 248.

p.43 ... *an abstract, depersonalizing rationalism.* Troeltsch, "Essence of Modern Spirit," 249.

p.43 ... *personal involvement with his product.* Troeltsch, "Essence of Modern Spirit," 247.

p.44 ... *and welfare departments on the other.* Lyon, 29.

p.44 ... *a process of* disremption. Habermas's German term is *Entzweiung*, which literally means "in-two-ness," or brokenness.

p.44 ... *the principle of subjectivity.* Habermas, 18.

p.44 ... *implicit and explicit.* Habermas, 41.

p.44 ... *and more aspects of life.* Lyon, 30.

p.45 ... *the discretion of trusted individuals.* D. West, 8.

p.45 ... *lines and spatial perspectives.* Max Weber, *The Protestant Ethic and the Spirit of Capitalism* [1904-05], trans. Talcott Parsons (New York: Routledge Press, 1992), 14.

p.45 ... *calculation underlies every single action.* Weber, 19.

p.45 ... *its own thought, institutions, and values.* D. West, 7.

p.45 ... *incapable of such development.* D. West, 9.

p.46 ... *the machine-like systems they now inhabit.* Lyon, 40.

p.48 ... *anything that contradicts our knowledge.* John Locke, *An Essay in Human Understanding* [1689], Book IV, chapter 18.

p.50 ... *to make room for* faith. Kant, *Critique*, 29 (italics in original).

p.50 ... *pretensions to transcendent insight.* Kant, *Critique*, 29.

p.51 ... *also not able to answer.* Kant, *Critique*, 7.

p.51 ... *human freedom and the existence of God.* There were three postulates, but the third is not necessary to our basic point and would complicate this discussion.

p.51 ... *moral judgments cannot be applied to them.* D. West, 24.

p.52 ... *the founding giants of liberal theology.* Gary Dorrien, *The Making of American Liberal Theology: Imagining Progressive Religion, 1805-1900* (Louisville, KY: Westminster John Knox, 2001), xvi.

p.54 ... *moral refinement requires education and training.* Dorrien, 14. For further discussion of the influence of Scottish commonsense philosophy on American liberal theology, see pp. 10-17, and Daniel Walker Howe, *The Unitarian Conscience: Harvard Moral Philosophy, 1805-1861* (Middletown, CT: Wesleyan University Press, 1988), 27-53.

p.55 ... *and New World slavery.* C. West, 52.

p.55 ... *torch of natural reason.* C. West, 51.

p.56 ... *normative gaze.* Cornel West, *Prophesy Deliverance! An Afro-American Revolutionary Christianity* (Philadelphia: Westminster Press, 1982), 53-65.

The Postmodern Challenge

p.57 ... *at the end of the twentieth century.* David Lyon, *Postmodernity,* 2nd ed. (Minneapolis: University of Minnesota Press, 1999), 1.

p.58 ... *it is like that.* Sallie McFague, *Life Abundant: Rethinking Theology and Economy for a Planet in Peril* (Minneapolis: Fortress Press, 2001), 181, quoting German philosopher Erich Heller.

p.59 ... *the toys that material success brings.* Paul Lakeland, *Postmodernity: Christian Identity in a Fragmented Age* (Minneapolis: Fortress Press, 1997), 8-9.

p.59 ... *what can be achieved is really quite limited.* Lakeland, 9.

p.59 ... *issue-specific political coalitions.* David Lyon, *Jesus in Disneyland: Religion in Postmodern Times* (Malden, MA: Polity Press, 2000), 54, quoting Princeton sociologist Pauline Rosenau.

p.60 ... *popular postmodern culture.* Lakeland, 9-10.

p.60 ... *sugar and preservatives.* Lakeland, 10.

p.60 ... *for their basic values.* Lakeland, 11.

p.61 ... *their postmodern world.* Lakeland, 11.

p.62 ... *while squatting in public squalor.* David Batstone, Eduardo Mendieta, Lois Ann Lorentzen, and Dwight N. Hopkins, eds., *Liberation Theologies, Postmodernity, and the Americas* (New York: Routledge Press, 1997), 7.

p.62 ... *time and space are in flux.* Lyon, *Jesus,* 12.

p.63 ...*generate what home-made authority it can.* Lyon, *Postmodernity*, 17.

p.63 ...*disappearance of historical teleology.* Anthony Giddens, *The Consequences of Modernity* (Stanford, CA: Stanford University Press, 1990), 52.

p.64 ...*Modernity is going nowhere.* Lyon, *Postmodernity*, 91.

p.65 ...*account for, and act in, the world.* Lyon, *Jesus*, 42.

p.65 ...*coming to terms with this.* Lyon, *Postmodernity*, 80.

p.65 ...*boundaries of what can be thought.* Lakeland, *Postmodernity*, 19.

p.66 ...*hierarchies of knowledge, taste, and opinion.* Lyon, *Postmodernity*, 10.

p.66 ...*'how do I choose?'* Lyon, *Jesus*, 43.

p.67 ...*which we shouldn't presume to do.* This controversy is treated in Bettina Shell-Duncan and Ylva Hernlund, eds., *Female "Circumcision" in Africa: Culture, Controversy, and Change* (Boulder, CO: Lynne Rienner, 2001). See also Alice Walker's novel *Possessing the Secret of Joy* (New York: Harcourt Brace Jovanovich, 1992).

p.67 ...*the voyages of Christopher Columbus.* See, for example, George E. Tinker, *Missionary Conquest: The Gospel and Native American Cultural Genocide* (Minneapolis: Fortress Press, 1993), vii.

p.68 ...*the last quarter of the twentieth century.* Lyon, *Jesus*, 7. Lyon here links consumerism and technology; he does not address violence. But it too is bound up with capitalism.

p.68 ...*in the sense that all are affected by it.* Lyon, *Postmodernity*, 88.

p.69 ...*displaces citizenship with consumership.* Lyon, *Jesus*, 12.

p.69 ...*participation in modern society.* Walter Wink, *Engaging the Powers: Discernment and Resistance in a World of Domination* (Minneapolis: Fortress Press, 1992), 54. While Wink uses the term *modern*, he is clearly thinking in terms of contemporary society, not modernity as used in this book.

p.69 ...*being a consumer is the determining factor.* Batstone, 6.

p.69 ...*boundless and useless consumption.* Batstone, 7.

p.70 ...*those who cannot afford to buy anything.* Batstone, 6.

p.70 ...*our cars tell the story of who we are (becoming).* Lyon, *Jesus*, 12.

p.71 ...*novel contexts of social interaction.* Lyon, *Jesus*, 13.

p.71 ...*political parties, nation states, or local communities.* Lyon, *Jesus*, 38.

p.72 ... *the real religion of America.* Wink, 13.

p.74 ... *reveal a structure of dominancy.* Max Weber, *Economy and Society,* 2nd ed. [1925] reprinted in Steven Lukes, ed., *Power: Readings in Social and Political Theory* (New York: New York University Press, 1986), 28, 29.

p.74 ... *Profit is the highest social good.* Wink, 54.

p.75 ... *toward total dominance and control.* Wendell Berry, "The Failure of War," reprinted in Philip Zaleski, ed., *The Best Spiritual Writing 2000* (New York: HarperCollins, 2000), 36-43.

p.75 ... *and liberation theologies.* Others have offered various organizing schemes; all share some parts of my classification. Examples include Lakeland, *Postmodernity*; Lyon, *Postmodernity*; Terrance W. Tilley, *Postmodern Theologies: The Challenge of Religious Diversity* (New York: Orbis Books, 1995); and James W. Fowler, *Faithful Change: The Personal and Public Challenges of Postmodern Life* (Nashville: Abington Press, 1996).

p.76 ... *with the fewest tents.* Lakeland, *Postmodernity*, 42.

p.77 ... *nontheological religious study.* See Mark C. Taylor, *Erring: A Postmodern A/Theology* (1984); *Disfiguring: Art, Architecture, Religion* (1992); *About Religion: Economies of Faith in Virtual Culture* (1999); all University of Chicago Press.

p.77 ... *in her first book.* Sharon D. Welch, *Communities of Resistance and Solidarity: A Feminist Theology of Liberation* (Maryknoll, NY: Orbis Books, 1985).

p.77 ... *spirituality without God.* Sharon D. Welch, *Sweet Dreams in America: Making Ethics and Spirituality Work* (New York: Routledge Press, 1999), xix.

p.77 ... *toward deconstructionist a/theology.* The author's article "The Postmodern Challenge to Liberal Theology," in *Unitarian Universalist Christian*, vol. 58 (2003), 5-56, notes that "Welch's postmodernism is not the postmodernism of the disengaged scholars who remain aloof from the struggle and play with texts in the safety of the academy. Welch is an involved academic, a scholar-activist whose work in many ways continues to follow the praxis-reflection model of liberation theology."

p.78 ... *consciously "writing against" it.* Lakeland, *Postmodernity*, 43.

p.78 ...*sprang onto the theological scene.* John Milbank, *Theology and Social Theory: Beyond Secular Reason* (Oxford, UK: Blackwell, 1990).

p.79 ...*faith and reason, grace and nature.* John Milbank, Catherine Pickstock, and Graham Ward, eds., *Radical Orthodoxy: A New Theology* (London: Routledge Press, 1999), 2.

p.79 ...*grounded literally in nothing.* Milbank, *Theology and Social Theory*, 3.

p.79 ...*superiority of Christendom.* Lakeland, *Postmodernity*, 68.

p.79 ...*theology as a metadiscourse.* Milbank, *Theology and Social Theory*, 1.

p.79 ...*the open court of reason.* Lakeland, *Postmodernity*, 72.

p.79 ...*religious activities, is simplistic.* James M. Gustafson, *An Examined Faith: The Grace of Self-Doubt* (Minneapolis: Fortress Press, 2004), 43.

p.80 ...*into a sectarian religion.* Gustafson, 44.

p.80 ...*the tide of theological liberalism.* Lakeland, *Postmodernity*, 65.

p.80 ...*a "cultural-linguistic" phenomenon.* George A. Lindbeck, *The Nature of Doctrine* (Philadelphia: Westminster, 1984).

p.81 ...*anthropologist Clifford Geertz and sociologist Peter Berger.* See Clifford Geertz, "Religion as a Cultural System," in *The Interpretation of Cultures* (New York: HarperCollins, 1973); Peter L. Berger and Thomas Luckmann, *The Social Construction of Reality* (New York: Doubleday, 1966); Peter L. Berger, *The Sacred Canopy: Elements of a Sociological Theory of Religion* (New York: Doubleday, 1967).

p.81 ...*the meaning a religion has for its adherents.* Lindbeck, 113.

p.81 ...*result in conservative stances.* Lindbeck, 126.

p.81 ...*modern expression of this view.* See Friedrich Schleiermacher, *The Christian Faith*, 2nd ed. [1830], eds. H. R. Macintosh and J. S. Stewart (Edinburgh: T. & T, Clark, 1989), 4.

p.81 ...*a particular quality of experience.* William James, *The Varieties of Religious Experience* [1902] (New York: Penguin Books, 1982), 31; John Dewey, *A Common Faith* (New Haven, CT: Yale University Press, 1934), 10.

p.82 ...*enjoining the golden rule.* Lakeland, *Postmodernity*, 65.

p.82 ...*that relativizes both modernity and postmodernity.* Lyon, *Postmodernity*, 108.

p.82 ...*Ernst Troeltsch, a century ago.* Ernst Troeltsch, "Historical and Dogmatic Method in Theology" [1898], in J. L. Adams and W. F. Bense, eds., *Religion in History* (Minneapolis: Fortress Press, 1991); Ernst

Troeltsch, *Christian Thought: Its History and Application*, F. von Hügel, ed. (London: University of London Press, 1923).

p.82 ... *before Lindbeck's model appeared.* See Gordon D. Kaufman, *Systematic Theology: A Historicist Perspective* (New York: Charles Scribner's Sons, 1968).

p.82 ... *simply take over traditional ideas.* Gordon D. Kaufman, *In Face of Mystery: A Constructive Theology* (Cambridge, MA: Harvard University Press, 1993), 29.

p.83 ... *through "continuing community."* Henry Nelson Wieman, *The Source of Human Good* (Carbondale: Southern Illinois University Press, 1946), 269.

p.84 ... *toothless in the face of oppression.* Batstone, 16.

The Problem of the Self

p.85 ... *our place in the scheme of things.* Sallie McFague, *The Body of God: An Ecological Theology* (Minneapolis: Fortress Press, 1993), 103.

p.86 ... *and breaking free.* See David West, *An Introduction to Continental Philosophy* (Cambridge, UK: Polity Press, 1996), 7-16.

p.86 ... *the survival of freedom itself.* Robert Bellah et al., *Habits of the Heart: Individualism and Commitment in American Life* (Berkeley: University of California Press, 1985), vii.

p.87 ... *social capital.* Robert Putnam, *Bowling Alone: The Collapse and Revival of American Community* (New York: Simon & Schuster, 2000), 19.

p.87 ... *shows how deeply individualism runs.* The survey results are published and analyzed in *Fulfilling the Promise*, 1998 report to the Unitarian Universalist Association General Assembly, 7-23.

p.88 ... *what is shared is still fundamentally individualistic.* Robert Bellah, "Unitarian Universalism in Societal Perspective," in *Fulfilling the Promise*, 10.

p.88 ... *independent of any churches or synagogues.* Bellah, *Habits of the Heart*, 228.

p.88 ... *any organizational involvement.* Bellah, *Habits of the Heart*, 226.

p.88 ... *the individual person.* Robert Bellah, "Is There a Common American Culture?" *Journal of the American Academy of Religion*, vol. 66 (1998): 613-625.

p.88 ... *society is secondary.* Bellah, "Unitarian Universalism," 15.

p.91 ... *social character of acquiring knowledge.* Cornel West, *Keeping Faith: Philosophy and Race in America* (New York: Routledge Press, 1993), 121-122.

p.92 ... *forces in man as well as without him.* John Dewey, *Human Nature and Conduct* [1922], ed. Jo Ann Boydston (Carbondale: Southern Illinois University Press, 1988), 9 (italics in original).

p.92 ... *before and after the fact.* Dewey, 16.

p.93 ... *to be assertive, insistent, self-perpetuating.* Dewey, 43.

p.93 ... *who is born into the world.* Dewey, 44.

p.93 ... *express itself in movement, come what may.* Michael G. Murphey, "Introduction," in Dewey, ix-xxiii.

p.94 ... *supplied by the social environment.* Dewey, 69.

p.94 ... *a matured social medium.* Dewey, 65 (italics added).

p.94 ... *whimsical contingency and lawful uniformity.* John Dewey, *Experience and Nature,* 2nd ed. [1929] (New York: Dover, 1958), 240.

p.94 ... *means of constructive growth.* Dewey, *Human Nature,* 68.

p.94 ... *an "original separate soul."* See Dewey, *Experience and Nature,* 219.

p.95 ... *"in process of making."* Dewey, *Human Nature,* 96.

p.95 ... *relationships to other selves.* George Herbert Mead, *Mind, Self, and Society,* ed. Charles W. Morris (Chicago: University of Chicago Press, 1934), 164.

p.96 ... *the individual and the community.* Mead, 215.

p.97 ... *outside of social experience.* Mead, 140.

p.97 ... *intersubjectively mediated self-understanding.* Jürgen Habermas, *Postmetaphysical Thinking: Philosophical Essays* (Cambridge, MA: MIT Press, 1993), 152-153.

p.97 ... *in the context of a shared lifeworld.* Johanna Meehan, "Autonomy, Recognition, and Respect: Habermas, Benjamin, and Honneth," in Johanna Meehan, ed., *Feminists Read Habermas: Gendering the Subject of Discourse* (New York: Routledge Press, 1995), 231-246.

p.98 ...*communicative competence.* See Jürgen Habermas, *Communication and the Evolution of Society* (Boston: Beacon Press, 1979), chapters 1 and 2.

p.98 ... *to standards of validity.* Allison Weir, "Toward a Model of Self-Identity: Habermas and Kristeva," in Meehan, 263-282.

p.99 ...*action to universal principles.* Jürgen Habermas, *The Theory of Communicative Action*, vol. 2 (Boston: Beacon Press, 1987), 97.

p.100 ...*as by biological evolution.* Gordon D. Kaufman, *In Face of Mystery: A Constructive Theology* (Cambridge: Harvard University Press, 1993), 117.

p.100 ... *"prolific cultural creativity."* Kaufman, 141.

p.100 ...*holds herself or himself accountable.* Kaufman, 147.

p.101 ...*as pictured by contemporary science.* McFague, 103.

p.101 ...*as pictured by postmodern science.* McFague, 103.

p.101 ...*the air, water, and soil.* McFague, 109.

p.102 ...*comes from interaction with it.* Sallie McFague, *Super, Natural Christians: How We Should Love Nature* (Minneapolis: Fortress Press, 1997), 99.

p.103 ...*the kinds of individuals we will become.* Seyla Benhabib, *Situating the Self: Gender, Community and Postmodernism in Contemporary Ethics* (New York: Routledge, 1992), 71.

p.104 ... *"material interaction at the most basic level."* Sharon D. Welch, *A Feminist Ethic of Risk* (Minneapolis: Fortress Press, 1990), 136.

p.105 ...*what is trivial and secondary.* Charles Taylor, *Sources of the Self: The Making of Modern Identity* (Cambridge: Harvard University Press, 1989), 28.

p.105 ...*communities, institutions, and systems of meaning.* Weir, 264.

p.106 ...*by those who bring us up.* Taylor, 35 (italics added).

Religious Experience and Language

p.110 ...*an experiential matter.* Wayne Proudfoot, *Religious Experience* (Berkeley: University of California Press, 1985), xi.

p.110 ...*its innermost essence known by them.* Friedrich Schleiermacher, *On Religion: Speeches to Its Cultured Despisers* [1799], trans. Richard Crouter (New York: Cambridge University Press, 1988), 95.

p.110 ...*but intuition and feeling.* Schleiermacher, 102.

p.111 ...*taste for the infinite.* Schleiermacher, 103.

p.111 ...*intuition of the universe.* Schleiermacher, 104.

p.111 ...*the infinite can be discovered.* Schleiermacher, 109.

p.111 ...*of being in relation with God.* Friedrich Schleiermacher, *The*

Christian Faith, 2nd ed. [1831], eds. H. R. Macintosh and J. S. Stewart (Edinburgh: T. & T. Clark, 1989), 4.

p.112 ... *inaccessible to thought and speech.* Thomas M. Kelly, *Theology at the Void: The Retrieval of Experience* (Notre Dame, IN: University of Notre Dame Press, 2002), 20.

p.112 ... *two different realities.* Kelly, 20.

p.112 ... *without having to desecrate it.* Schleiermacher, *On Religion*, 112.

p.113 ... *the doctrines cannot arise.* Schleiermacher, *Christian Faith*, 15.

p.113 ... *clarification of believing experience.* Richard R. Niebuhr, *Schleiermacher on Christ and Religion* (New York: Charles Scribner's Sons, 1964), 139.

p.113 ... *whatever they may consider divine.* William James, *The Varieties of Religious Experience* [1902] (New York: Penguin Books, 1982), 31.

p.113 ... *what we may call 'something there.'* James, 58.

p.113 ... *"gone to pieces in the wreck."* James, 508.

p.114 ... *personal religion pure and simple.* James, 29.

p.114 ... *mystical states of consciousness.* James, 379.

p.114 ... *the quality or worth of it consists.* James, 380.

p.114 ... *ecclesiastical organizations may secondarily grow.* James, 31.

p.114 ... *could ever have been framed.* James, 431.

p.115 ... *conflicts of historical strife.* Nancy Frankenberry, "Major Themes of Empirical Theology," in Randolph Crump Miller, ed., *Empirical Theology: A Handbook* (Birmingham, AL: Religious Education Press, 1992), 36-56.

p.116 ... *the reality of religious experience.* Henry Nelson Wieman, *Religious Experience and Scientific Method* (New York: Macmillan, 1926), 29.

p.116 ... *which constantly overflows one.* Wieman, 38, 39.

p.117 ... *we have no religion at all.* Wieman, 41.

p.118 ... *he advances somewhat beyond it.* Henry Nelson Wieman, *Man's Ultimate Commitment* (Carbondale: Southern Illinois University Press, 1958), 88.

p.118 ... *help guide our interpretive efforts.* Henry Nelson Wieman, *Religious Inquiry: Some Explorations* (Boston: Beacon Press, 1968), 11-12.

p.118 ...*constructs of the human imagination.* Sallie McFague, *The Body of God: An Ecological Theology* (Minneapolis: Fortress Press, 1993), 86.

p.119 ...*creatures like and unlike ourselves.* McFague, 86.

p.119 ...*both constructed and both particular.* McFague, 87.

p.120 ...*social community of actual language users.* Seyla Benhabib, *Situating the Self: Gender, Community, and Postmodernism in Contemporary Ethics* (New York: Routledge Press, 1992), 209. For an excellent summary of Wittgenstein's theory of language, see John B. Thompson, *Critical Hermeneutics: A Study in the Thought of Paul Ricoeur and Jürgen Habermas* (Cambridge, UK: Cambridge University Press, 1981), 12-23.

p.122 ...*all perception is always already interpretation.* Gayle L. Ormiston and Alan D. Schrift, "Editor's Introduction," in Gayle L. Ormiston and Alan D. Schrift, eds., *The Hermeneutical Tradition* (Albany: State University of New York Press, 1990), 16.

p.122 ...*a historically situated, intersubjective lifeworld.* David West, *An Introduction to Continental Philosophy* (Cambridge, UK: Polity Press, 1996), 108.

p.122 ...*the dimension of history and tradition.* West, 162.

p.123 ...*through the languages available to us.* David Tracy, *Plurality and Ambiguity: Hermeneutics, Religion, Hope* (Chicago: The University of Chicago Press, 1987), 48.

p.123 ...*more than it belongs to me.* Tracy, 49-50.

p.123 ...*viewed as derivative.* George Lindbeck, *The Nature of Doctrine* (Philadelphia: Westminster, 1984), 34.

p.123 ...*use the appropriate symbol systems.* Lindbeck, 34

p.123 ...*boundaries of what can be thought.* Paul Lakeland, *Postmodernity: Christian Identity in a Fragmented Age* (Minneapolis: Fortress, 1997), 19.

p.123 ...*far more than sensation.* Susanne K. Langer, *Philosophy in a New Key: A Study in the Symbolism of Reason, Rite, and Art* (New York: Mentor Books, 1951), 34.

p.124 ...*knowledge about and attitudes toward life.* Clifford Geertz, *The Interpretation of Cultures* (New York: HarperCollins, 1973), 89.

p.124 ...*they are prerequisites of it.* Geertz, 49.

p.125 ...*as the self is created.* Gordon D. Kaufman, *In Face of Mystery: A Constructive Theology* (Cambridge, MA: Harvard University Press, 1933), 347.

p.125 ... *principle of experience.* Kaufman, 167.

p.125 ... *an experience of that meaning.* Francis Schüssler Fiorenza, *Foundational Theology: Jesus and the Church* (New York: Crossroad Press, 1992), 300.

p.126 ... *beliefs, grammatical rules, and practices.* Proudfoot, 228.

p.126 ... *formative role in religious experience.* Proudfoot, 40.

p.126 ... *a consciousness of God.* Schleiermacher, *Christian Faith*, 17-18.

p.127 ... *particular concepts, beliefs, and practices.* Proudfoot, xv-xvi.

p.127 ... *were made manifest to me.* James, 293.

p.127 ... *no longer felt any difficulty.* James, 403.

p.128 ... *perceived, examined, described, interpreted.* Kaufman, 13.

p.128 ... *is possible for us.* Kaufman, 333.

p.129 ... *moving from "experience" to theology.* Kaufman, 22.

p.129 ... *more problems that it has solved.* Frankenberry, 50.

p.129 ... *"religious experience" understood individualistically.* Frankenberry, 50.

p.130 ... *data given directly and immediately.* Gordon D. Kaufman, "Empirical Realism in Theology: An Examination of Some Themes in Meland and Loomer," in W. Creighton Peden and Larry E. Axel, eds., *New Essays in Religious Naturalism* (Macon, GA: Mercer University Press, 1993), 135-160.

p.130 ... *which they in fact always are.* Kaufman, "Empirical Realism," 135-136.

p.131 ... *well-clothed sisters and brothers.* McFague, 48. For further development of the idea of embodiment in theology, see Thandeka, "The Self Between Feminist Theory and Theology," in Rebecca S. Chopp and Sheila Greeve Davaney, eds., *Horizons in Feminist Theology: Identity, Tradition, and Norms* (Minneapolis: Fortress Press, 1997), 79-98.

p.131 ... *we are embodied beings.* See Kaufman, *In Face of Mystery*, 154-155.

p.131 ... *thoroughly constructive character.* Kaufman, "Empirical Realism," 146.

p.133 ... *characterize evangelical Christianity.* Nancy Frankenberry, *Religion and Radical Empiricism* (Albany: State University of New York Press, 1987), 13. Not all evangelical Christianity is dogmatic or conservative in the sense Frankenberry is describing here. As noted earlier, there is a strong evangelical strand within liberal theology itself. A better term would have been *fundamentalism.*

p.133 ... *rich forms of embodiment.* McFague, 86.

p.134 ... *efforts at expressing their experiences?* McFague, 240, fn. 56.

p.134 ... *frameworks that are more persuasive.* McFague, 42.

p.135 ... *will better fit that experience.* Kaufman, *In Face of Mystery,* 51.

p.136 ... *the causality is reciprocal.* Lindbeck, 33.

p.136 ... *viewed as the leading partners.* Lindbeck, 34.

p.136 ... *must be emphasized.* Kelly, 113.

p.136 ... *a careful and nuanced both/and.* Kelly, 138.

Liberation Theology

p.141 ... *profound critique of liberal theology.* This chapter draws primarily on Latin American liberation theology because of the author's experiences in Central America during the 1980s. However, other liberation perspectives are also addressed, including feminist liberation theology and black liberation theology.

p.142 ... *the possibility of class, racial, and sexual equality.* Cornel West, *The Cornel West Reader* (New York: Basic Civitas Books, 1999), 393.

p.142 ... *in which God reveals (it)self.* Franz J. Hinkelhammert, "Liberation Theology in the Economic and Social Context of Latin America: Economy and Theology, or the Irrationality of the Rationalized," in David Batstone, Eduardo Mendieta, Lois Ann Lorentzen, and Dwight N. Hopkins, eds., *Liberation Theologies, Postmodernity, and the Americas* (New York: Routledge Press, 1997), 25-52.

p.143 ... *the deposit of faith.* Clodovis Boff, "Methodology of Liberation Theology," in Jon Sobrino and Ignacia Ellacuría, eds., *Systematic Theology: Perspectives from Liberation Theology* (Maryknoll, NY: Orbis, 1996), 1-21.

p.143 ... *"preferential option for the poor."* See Gustavo Gutiérrez, "Option for the Poor," in ibid. 22-37.

p.143 ... *against the pharaohs of this world.* Leonardo Boff and Clodovis Boff, *Introducing Liberation Theology* (Maryknoll, NY: Orbis Books, 1987), 50.

p.143 ... *"What is ultimate in Christian faith?"* Jon Sobrino, "Central

Position of the Reign of God in Liberation Theology," in Sobrino and Ellacuría, op cit. 38-74.

p.143 ... *the divine predilection for "history's last."* Gutiérrez, 26.

p.144 ... *what love and hope are, and so on.* Sobrino, 39.

p.144 ... *makes life and dignity possible for the poor.* Sobrino, 52, 56.

p.144 ... *the poor as a social phenomenon.* Boff and Boff, 32.

p.144 ... *poor because of injustice.* Sobrino, 55.

p.145 ... *sophisticated skepticism of the educated classes.* Harvey Cox, *Religion in the Secular City: Toward a Postmodern Theology* (New York: Simon and Schuster, 1984), 164.

p.145 ... *prisms of oppression/liberation and idolatry/God of life.* Eduardo Mendieta, "From Christendom to Polycentric Oikonumé: Modernity, Postmodernity, and Liberation Theology," in Batstone, 253-272.

p.145 ... *liberation theology's methodology.* Boff and Boff, chapter 3; Francis Schüssler Fiorenza, "Systematic Theology: Task and Methods," in F. S. Fiorenza and J. P. Galvin, eds., *Systematic Theology: Roman Catholic Perspectives*, vol. 1 (Minneapolis: Fortress Press, 1991).

p.147 ... *Latin America, for example.* See Gustavo Gutiérrez, *A Theology of Liberation*, rev. ed. (Maryknoll, NY: Orbis Books, 1988), chapter 2.

p.147 ... *unemployment and class inequality.* Cornel West, *Prophesy Deliverance! An Afro-American Revolutionary Christianity* (Philadelphia: Westminster Press, 1982), 143.

p.147 ... *a form of "institutionalized violence."* Gutiérrez, *Theology of Liberation*, xxi.

p.147 ... *deep-seated structures of patriarchy and racism.* See Elisabeth Schüssler Fiorenza, *Bread Not Stone: The Challenge of Feminist Biblical Interpretation* (Boston: Beacon Press, 1984), chapter 1; West, *Prophesy Deliverance!*, chapter 2.

p.148 ... *a mutual acknowledgment between subjects.* Hinkelhammert, 26.

p.148 ... *wherever this acknowledgement [between subjects] occurs.* Hinkelhammert, 26-27.

p.148 ... *the absence of God.* Hinkelhammert, 17.

p.148 ... *a doing, a praxis.* Hinkelhammert, 27.

p.149 ... *and hopes of the poor.* Boff and Boff, 32.

p.149 ... *such as women's voices, are recovered.* See Elisabeth Schüssler Fiorenza, *In Memory of Her: A Feminist Theological Reconstruction of Christian Origins* (New York: Crossroad, 1989).

p.150 ...*experienced in the Third World.* Boff and Boff, 34.

p.150 ...*what the text means to the poor.* Cox, 154.

p.151 ...*establish what the Bible really says.* Cox, 168 (italics in original).

p.152 ...*in terms of their impact on the poor.* National Conference of Catholic Bishops, *Economic Just for All: Pastoral Letter on Catholic Social Teaching and the U.S. Economy* (Washington, DC: National Conference of Catholic Bishops, 1986), x-xi.

p.153 ...*to be fully human beings?* Dwight N. Hopkins, *Introducing Black Theology of Liberation* (Maryknoll, NY: Orbis Books, 1999), 4.

p.153 ...*speeches, deeds, and actions.* Peter J. Paris, *The Social Teaching of the Black Churches* (Philadelphia: Fortress Press, 1985), xiii.

p.153 ...*churches of the nineteenth century.* Paris, xiii.

p.153 ...*is possible in this nation.* Paris, 33.

p.154 ...*on economic power in 1969.* These and other important documents can be found in Gayraud S. Wilmore and James H. Cone, eds., *Black Theology: A Documentary History*, 2 vols. (Maryknoll, NY: Orbis, 1979 and 1993).

p.154 ...*black liberation theology movement.* C. Eric Lincoln and Lawrence H. Mamiya, *The Black Church in the African American Experience* (Durham, NC: Duke University Press, 1990), especially chapter 7. Rural churches were not included in the study.

p.154 ...*"alien to the black church tradition."* Paris, xv.

p.154 ...*to liberate the poor.* Hopkins, 4.

p.154 ...*racial injustice...initiated in the black churches.* James H. Cone, *For My People: Black Theology and the Black Church* (Maryknoll, NY: Orbis, 1984), 6.

p.155 ...*separation from God as well.* Joerg Rieger, *Remember the Poor: The Challenge to Theology in the Twenty-First Century* (Harrisburg, PA: Trinity Press, 1998), 16-17.

p.155 ...*functions in liberal theology.* A more detailed treatment of the role of experience in liberal theology is offered in the previous chapter.

p.157 ...*developments in black culture.* See Hopkins, 65-84.

p.157 ...*for liberation theology's orthopraxis, is God's will.* Hinkelhammert, 27.

p.158 ...*when theory meets practice.* Batstone, 14.

p.158 ...*technical or artistic production (techne)*. Aristotle, *Nicomachean Ethics*, trans. Martin Ostwald (Englewood Cliffs, NJ: Prentice Hall, 1962), Book VI.

p.158 ...*a question of theory*. Karl Marx, *Theses on Feuerbach* [1845], in *Selected Writings*, ed. David McLellan (New York: Oxford University Press, 1977), 156-158.

p.158 ...*between ideology and social structure*. Karl Marx and Friedrich Engles, *The German Ideology* [1845], in ibid., 159-191.

p.159 ...*life as fundamentally practical*. Rebecca Chopp, *The Praxis of Suffering: An Interpretation of Liberation and Political Theologies* (Maryknoll, NY: Orbis Books, 1986), 37.

p.159 ...*back again to changed praxis*. Dorothee Sölle, *Thinking About God: An Introduction to Theology*, trans. John Bowden (Valley Forge, PA: Trinity Press International, 1990), 6.

p.159 ...*dangerous political tasks*. Cox, 136.

p.159 ...*and theological reflection a tinkling cymbal*. West, 398.

p.160 ...*we may respond to suffering*. Chopp, 122.

p.160 ...*struggle for autonomy*. Rieger, 18.

p.160 ...*an ideology for the bourgeois*. Chopp, 26.

p.160 ...*as objects of charity*. Sölle, 17-18.

p.160 ...*an ethic of individual responsibility*. H. Richard Niebuhr, *The Social Sources of Denominationalism* (New York: Holt, 1929), especially chapter 4.

p.160 ...*of partial social change*. Sharon D. Welch, *A Feminist Ethic of Risk* (Minneapolis: Fortress Press, 1990), 15.

p.161 ...*the power struggle of the modern world*. Rieger, 20.

p.161 ...*members of the same body*. Robert Bellah, "Unitarian Universalism in Societal Perspective," in *Fulfilling the Promise*, 1998 report to the Unitarian Universalist Association General Assembly, 7-23.

p.161 ... *"enormous cultural consequences."* Bellah, 16, 17.

p.161 ...*connectedness to the other*. Rieger, 27.

p.162 ...*co-constituitive as oneself*. Frederick Herzog, "Jesus and Power," in *Philosophy of Religion and Theology: 1975 Proceedings*, American Academy of Religion Section Papers, ed. James Wm. McClendon Jr. (Missoula, MT: Scholars Press, 1975), 207; quoted in ibid., 28.

p.162 ... *bring the subject to historical accountability.* Batstone, 14.

p.162 ... *class conversion.* Boff and Boff, 23.

The Challenge of Racism

p.166 ... *rather than radical social change.* H. Richard Niebuhr, *Christ and Culture* (New York: Harper and Row, 1951), 84.

p.166 ... *the political and cultural status quo.* Cornel West, *Prophetic Fragments: Illuminations of the Crisis in American Religion and Culture* (Grand Rapids, MI: W.B. Eerdmans, 1988), ix.

p.166 ... *the altars erected by American culture.* West, ix.

p.166 ... *an ethic of individual responsibility.* See H. Richard Niebuhr, *The Social Sources of Denominationalism* (New York: Holt, 1929), especially chapter 4.

p.167 ... *groups rising to power in a civilization.* Niebuhr, *Christ and Culture*, 104.

p.167 ... *let alone feelings of self-worth.* Parker J. Palmer, *The Promise of Paradox: A Celebration of Contradictions in the Christian Life* (Washington, DC: The Servant Leadership School, 1993), 26.

p.168 ... *for adjustment and reformulation.* Sidney E. Ahlstrom, *A Religious History of the American People* (New Haven, CT: Yale University Press, 1972), 767.

p.169 ... *survival of the fittest.* Gary Dorrien, *The Making of American Liberal Theology, vol. 1: Imagining Progressive Religion, 1805-1900* (Louisville, KY: Westminster John Knox, 2001), 315.

p.169 ... *the way the world works.* Dorrien, 315.

p.170 ... *humanity civilized and Christian.* Dorrien, 320.

p.170 ... *book of the nineteenth century.* Ahlstrom, 798.

p.170 ... *it has Anglo-Saxonized mankind?* From Strong's 1893 book *The New Era; or, The Coming Kingdom*, quoted in Ahlstrom, 849.

p.170 ... *pervaded nineteenth-century American society.* Dorrien, xix.

p.171 ... *superficial and often patronizing.* Gary Dorrien, *The Making of American Liberal Theology, vol. 2: Idealism, Realism, and Modernity, 1900-1950* (Louisville, KY: Westminster John Knox, 2003), 430.

p.171 ... *a whiff of white supremacy.* Dorrien, vol. 2, 431.

p.172 ... *often casually racist.* Dorrien, vol. 2, 430.

p.172 ... *as Martin Luther King Jr. frequently observed.* Dorrien, vol. 2, 557.

p.173 ...*the 1965 Voting Rights Act.* Anthony E. Cook, *The Least of These: Race, Law, and Religion in American Culture* (New York: Routledge Press, 1997), 161.

p.173 ...*freedom for the black poor.* James H. Cone, *Martin & Malcolm & America: A Dream or a Nightmare* (Maryknoll, NY: Orbis, 1991), 233.

p.173 ...*first to attack this evil.* James H. Cone, "Theology's Great Sin: Silence in the Face of White Supremacy," in Marjorie Bowens-Wheatley and Nancy Palmer Jones, eds., *Soul Work: Anti-Racist Theologies in Dialogue* (Boston: Skinner House, 2003), 1-17.

p.174 ...*resent being labeled racists.* Cone, "Theology's Great Sin," 8.

p.174 ...*structures of power remain intact.* Cone, "Theology's Great Sin," 12.

p.174 ...*with their stories of hurt.* Cone, "Theology's Great Sin," 8.

p.174 ...*not to identify with black suffering.* Cone, "Theology's Great Sin," 9.

p.175 ...*rage for their social taste.* Cone, "Theology's Great Sin," 9.

p.175 ...*white scholars of religion is long overdue.* Cone, "Theology's Great Sin," 13-14.

p.175 ...*one promising sign.* Cone, "Theology's Great Sin," 5.

p.176 ...*truly tempting our despair.* Billy Wylie-Kellermann, "Exorcising an American Demon," *Sojourners* (March-April 1998).

p.177 ...*unconscious enthrallment as well.* Walter Wink, *Unmasking the Powers: The Invisible Forces That Determine Human Existence* (Philadelphia: Fortress Press, 1986), 67-68.

p.177 ...*necessary for spiritual transformation.* Cook, 113, discussing Martin Luther King Jr.'s conception of the Beloved Community.

p.177 ...*knows nothing about.* Walter Wink, *Engaging the Powers: Discernment and Resistance in a World of Domination* (Minneapolis: Fortress Press, 1992), 10.

p.178 ...*is threatened by community.* Cook, 141.

p.179 ...*it's people I can't stand.* Robert L. Short, *The Gospel According to Peanuts* (Richmond, VA: John Knox, 1965), 122.

p.179 ...*at the core of their programs.* These theological options are discussed in more detail in "The Postmodern Challenge" section.

p.180 ...*and ways of balancing power.* Sharon D. Welch, *Sweet Dreams in America: Making Ethics and Spirituality Work* (New York: Routledge Press, 1999), 48.

p.180 ... *values, practices, and history.* Welch, 53.

p.180 ... *How much critique?* Welch, 55.

p.181 ... *the shock of difference.* Welch, 61.

p.181 ... *difference that enriches life.* Welch, 62.

p.181 ... *acts of worship that feed the soul.* Sharon D. Welch, "Human Beings, White Supremacy, and Racial Justice," in Rebecca S. Chopp and Mark Lewis Taylor, eds., *Reconstructing Christian Theology* (Minneapolis: Fortress Press, 1994), 170-94, 191.

p.181 ... *the intransigence of structures of oppression.* Sharon D. Welch, *A Feminist Ethic of Risk* (Minneapolis: Fortress Press, 1990), 136.

p.182 ... *the role of the faith community.* Paul Lakeland, *Postmodernity: Christian Identity in a Fragmented Age* (Minneapolis: Fortress Press, 1997), 58.

p.182 ... *as important as political praxis.* Lakeland, 63.

p.183 ... *in an extensive community.* Welch, *Feminist Ethic of Risk,* 21.

p.183 ... *our own capitulation to structured evil.* Welch, *Feminist Ethic of Risk,* 22.

For Further Reading

Liberal Theology and Liberal Religion in General

Ahlstrom, Sydney E. *A Religious History of the American People.* New Haven, CT: Yale University Press, 1972.

Dorrien, Gary. *The Making of American Liberal Theology: Imagining Progressive Religion 1805-1900.* Louisville, KY: Westminster John Knox, 2001.

——. *The Making of American Liberal Theology: Idealism, Realism, and Modernity 1900–1950.* Louisville, KY: Westminster John Knox, 2003.

——. *The Making of American Liberal Theology: Crisis, Irony, and Postmodernity 1950–2004.* Louisville, KY: Westminster John Knox, 2006.

Gustafson, James M. *An Examined Faith: The Grace of Self-Doubt.* Minneapolis: Fortress, 2004.

Welch, Claude. *Protestant Thought in the Nineteenth Century*, 2 vols. New Haven, CT: Yale University Press, 1972-1985.

Philosophical Roots of Liberal Theology, Modernity

Spretnak, Charlene. *The Resurgence of the Real: Body, Nature, and Place in a Hypermodern World.* Reading, MA: Addison-Wesley, 1997.

Taylor, Charles. *Sources of the Self: The Making of Modern Identity.* Cambridge: Harvard University Press, 1989.

Troeltsch, Ernst. *Protestantism and Progress: The Significance of Protestantism for the Rise of the Modern World.* 1912. Philadelphia: Fortress, 1986.

West, David. *An Introduction to Continental Philosophy.* Cambridge, UK: Polity Press, 1996.

Postmodernity and Postmodern Theologies

Lakeland, Paul. *Postmodernity: Christian Identity in a Fragmented Age.* Minneapolis: Fortress, 1997.

Lyon, David. *Postmodernity,* 2nd ed. Minneapolis: University of Minnesota Press, 1999.

——————. *Jesus in Disneyland: Religion in Postmodern Times.* Malden, MA: Polity Press, 2000.

Tilley, Terrance W. *Postmodern Theologies: The Challenge of Religious Diversity.* New York: Orbis Books, 1995.

Religious Experience

James, William. *The Varieties of Religious Experience.* 1902. New York: Penguin Books, 1982.

Kelly, Thomas M. *Theology at the Void: The Retrieval of Experience.* Notre Dame, IN: University of Notre Dame Press, 2002.

Proudfoot, Wayne. *Religious Experience.* Berkeley: University of California Press, 1985.

Liberation Theology

Boff, Leonardo and Clodovis. *Introducing Liberation Theology.* Maryknoll, NY: Orbis Books, 1987.

Chopp, Rebecca. *The Praxis of Suffering: An Interpretation of Liberation and Political Theologies.* Maryknoll, NY: Orbis Books, 1986.

Gutiérrez, Gustavo. *A Theology of Liberation.* Rev. ed. Maryknoll, NY: Orbis Books, 1988.

Sobrino, Jon and Ignacia Ellacuría, eds. *Systematic Theology: Perspectives from Liberation Theology.* Maryknoll, NY: Orbis Books, 1996.

Theology and Race

Bowens-Wheatley, Marjorie and Nancy Palmer Jones, eds. *Soul Work: Anti-Racist Theologies in Dialogue.* Boston: Skinner House, 2003.

Cone, James H. *God of the Oppressed.* Rev. ed. Maryknoll, NY: Orbis Books, 1997.

Cook, Anthony E. *The Least of These: Race, Law, and Religion in American Culture.* New York: Routledge, 1997.

Hopkins, Dwight N. *Introducing Black Theology of Liberation.* Maryknoll, NY: Orbis Books, 1999.

Thandeka, *Learning to be White: Money, Race, and God in America.* New York: Continuum, 1999.

Tinker, George E. *Missionary Conquest: The Gospel and Native American Cultural Genocide.* Minneapolis: Fortress, 1993.

West, Cornel. *Prophesy Deliverance! An Afro-American Revolutionary Christianity.* Philadelphia: Westminster Press, 1982.

Index

Abbot, Francis Ellingwood, 13–14
Scientific Theism, 14, 169
Abrams, M.H., on metaphysics of integration, 16
Adams, James Luther, 156
on continuous recreation of reality, 21
on human freedom, 23–24
on liberal commitment to openness, xi
on liberal mind-set, 2
on progressive element in religious liberalism, xii
on social action and power, 28–29
"Theological Bases of Social Action," 29
on voluntary associations, 29
African Methodist Episcopal Church, 153
Age of Reason. *See* Enlightenment
Ahlstrom, Sidney
on Abbot, 14
on Darwin, 168
on golden age of American liberal theology, 7
Anthropology, theological, 85
Applied theology, 159
Aristotle, definition of praxis, 158
Art(s)
and liberal theology, 13
and orientation in world, xvi

rationalization and, 45
subjectivity and, 35
Astronomy, and orientation in world, xvi
Authority
of church, 34
external
liberal religious mind-set and, 22–23
modern challenge to, 33, 35–36, 40–41, 53, 82
of individual, 35–36
theological, sources of, in liberation theology, 149–158
Autonomy
individual, 85–86
liberal doctrine of, xi, 22–24, 26
loss of, rationalization and, 46
postconventional perspective on, 99
social self and, 107–108

Barth, Karl, 7, 78
Batstone, David
on consumerism, 68
on postmodernity, 61–62
on postmodernity and oppression, 83–84
Bellah, Robert
Habits of the Heart, 86, 88

217